Happy Birthday Bri
I love this
I all happy
where I was
getting ann
Bob out, you'll
have to come
join us
sometime

Jane Faulkner
Adkins

Graveyard of Dreams

Dashed Hopes and Shattered Aspirations
Along Alaska's Iditarod Trail

by
Craig Medred

Plaid Cabin
PUBLISHING

Plaid Cabin Publishing
18130 Norway Drive
Anchorage, Alaska 99516

This title was first published in May 2010 by Plaid Cabin Publishing.

This is a work of nonfiction. Names, characters, places and incidents happened during the running of the 2010 Iditarod Trail Sled Dog Race from Anchorage to Nome. News coverage of these Iditarod stories from the 2010 race can be found at
www.alaskadispatch.com

This book may be purchased in quantity for resale, education, business or promotional uses. For information about purchasing, contact Publisher, Plaid Cabin Publishing, 18130 Norway Drive, Anchorage, Alaska 99516.

Excerpts from *To The Man on Trail*, a short story by Jack London, copyright © 1900 by Jack London, are taken from the *Overland Monthly* published in January 1899.

FIRST EDITION

Printed in the United States of America

Cover Design: Aaron Jansen
Book Design and Layout: TerraGraphica
Photography: Katie Medred, Craig Medred and Stephen Nowers

ISBN 978-0-615-36043-0
Graveyard of Dreams: Dashed Hopes and Shattered Aspirations
Along Alaska's Iditarod Trail / Craig Medred

Family – Adventure Sports – Interpersonal Relations

"So, a health to the man on trail this night;
may his grub hold out; may his dogs keep their legs;
may his matches never miss fire. God prosper him;
good luck go with him...."

~ Malemute Kid
"To the Man on Trail," Jack London
Overland Monthly, January 1899

The Iditarod Trail

Northern Route

NOME

SAFETY

GOLOVIN

WHITE MOUNTAIN

ELIM

KOYUK

NULATO

SHAKTOOLIK

KALTAG

UNALAKLEET

NORTON SOUND

YUKON RIVER

KUSKOKWIM RIVER

KOYUKUK RIVER

LENA

RUBY

YUKON RIVER

NENANA RIVER

NENANA

CRIPPLE

OPHIR

TAKOTNA

MCGRATH

NIKOLAI

ROHN

RAINY PASS

FINGER LAKE

SKWENTNA

WILLOW

YENTNA

ANCHORAGE

Acknowledgements

Writing a work of nonfiction like this is simple. You venture afield, feast on the nectar of human drama, return to the hive, slit open a vein and bleed the stories onto the appropriate pages. The bleeding part is easy; we all bleed. More difficult, far more difficult in this particular case, was the collection of the raw material. That required the help of many, and to all of them I am greatly thankful.

To Robbie Graham, who first encouraged me to crawl out from beneath the dying carcass of newspaper journalism and then provided editorial, emotional and financial support when I found it impossible to shake the addiction to a lifetime of reportage. Thus began a crazy new adventure to do the same old thing in an entirely different way.

To Tony Hopfinger and Alice Rogoff at www.AlaskaDispatch.com whose response to my off-the-wall suggestion that someone cover the back of the pack in the Iditarod Trail Sled Dog Race by snowmachine was simple: Do it. Many of the stories that appear in this book appeared in their first draft on AlaskaDispatch.com. Without the financial support provided by Dispatch for this adventure, it is unlikely this book would have been written.

To Dudley Benesch and Steve Herschbach at Alaska Mining & Diving Supply, and by association BRP Ski-doo, for the loan of the Tundra II LT snowmachine that made the journey possible. I'm not sure anyone in this group received much out of the adventure by way of advertising, but they have my gratitude and they can take a little pride in playing a role in helping to tell what I hope are some fine Alaska stories.

To Dave Karp and Margot Wiegele at Northern Air Cargo who probably earned even less in the way of advertising out of this crazy undertaking, but who graciously agreed to fly the Skidoo and a sled back to Anchorage anyway. I can only attribute this to the fact that Dave, like Dudley and Steve, is a son of Alaska, and there is in all sons of Alaska a great love for the frontier and the stories that have long been associated with it.

To Steve Yeatts at Rhodes Communications in Virginia who arranged for the loan of an Iridium satellite phone with which to Twitter from the trail, maintain contact with the office and provide some sort of backup in case of breakdown. I anticipated that at some point during the 1,000-mile odyssey to Nome the phone would be needed to call for an airdrop of supplies or to fix something, but the Ski-doo Tundra overcame all the punishment of my sometimes less than skillful driving. Thus I was relegated to using the device to call and harass journalistic friends bound to desk jobs where reporting has become all too much about taking phone calls and making up much to fill in for what one has never seen.

To the legions of good folks who provided support along the trail in one way or another. I am almost afraid to start naming them for fear the many left out might feel slighted.

Graveyard of Dreams

But Bill Merchant of the Iditarod Invitational warrants special mention for the loan of his toboggan for hauling gear, along with Dan and Jean Gabryszak at Yentna Station Roadhouse for their always warm welcome and support. Likewise for Norma and Joe Delia in Skwentna and Bonnie Childs at the Skwentna Roadhouse, and Carl Dixon, his family and the whole staff at Winterlake Lodge; there is no place the man on the trail gets a better welcome.

But there are many places where people try with whatever means at their disposal. So here's to Jasper Bond and Terry Boyle for keeping the Rohn cabin warm and a long-overdue thanks from another time for keeping me filled with Theraflu for a few days when I thought I might die there; Scott Studie in Nikolai for opening the school and helping me figure out how to get a computer connection; the whole community of McGrath for its embrace of Iditarod and any bum who happens to be moving north with it; Jan and Dick Newton and the rest of the crew in Takotna for a hearty meal and good conversation; Jim and Bill Gallea for keeping the tents of the almost-nothing Cripple checkpoint warm and the mood there uplifting at 50 degrees below zero; Jimmy Honea, Kevin Saiki, Emmitt Peters and the good ladies of Ruby for their support along the Yukon River; Larry Esmailka in Nulato for offering a warm place to sleep and contributing a wonderful explanation of the Stick Dance Festival; Bret Hanscom at Peace on Earth pizza in Unalakleet for volunteering an internet connection in his kitchen in a pinch and more for sending a free pizza out the road to cheer dejected musher Hank Debruin after he quit the race; Paul Nagaruk in Elim for loaning me his drill to make repairs on the toboggan after it broke out on the sea ice (the drill bits I promised are on the way, buddy); mushers too many to name who were always friendly and willing to talk no matter how bad things were going for them; and last, but certainly not least, the many Iditarod volunteers – often namelessly passed in the night – in villages from Nikolai north who offered a place to warm my frostbitten nose or pointed me in the direction of a hot cup of coffee. Thanks to you all.

Finally, a few words must be offered in honor of all of those long gone from the scene who went before to make the Iditarod the wonderful madness that it is, from Joe Redington to Susan Butcher to the old Shishmaref Cannonball Herbie Nayokpuk and young Howard Albert, who I miss much. Not to mention those who enrich the trail still and will come to leave their mark in the future: They are wonderful characters all.

"So a health to the man on trail this night," as Jack London, a far better writer than I, let the Malemute Kid shout out in a short story published in 1899, "may his grub hold out; may his dogs keep their legs; may his matches never miss fire. God prosper him; good luck go with him...."

Introduction

Long before there was an Iditarod Trail Sled Dog Race, there was an Iditarod Trail. It began not in the sprawling metropolis of Anchorage, Alaska, where the Iditarod race starts today, but in the small town of Seward at the head of ice-free Resurrection Bay. From there, the trail stretched for 900 miles through the ranges of the Kenai, Chugach and Alaska mountains into the vast frozen Interior and onto the Bering Sea coast and the fabled golden city of Nome.

Dreamers by the thousands traveled up that trail. They came on foot, on snowshoes, on skis, occasionally on bicycles and often on the runners of sleds behind dog teams, all chasing visions of gold in the hills, gold in the creeks and gold in the sands of the Nome beaches. Few found much in the way of riches. Many were forced to bury their dreams along the way.

Between 1910 and 1912, an estimated 10,000 people stormed north to the communities of Flat, Ophir, Ruby and other specks on Alaska's map acting as towns in pursuit of the Iditarod gold rush. Over the next two decades, $30 million in gold was flushed out of the ground there. It made a few people rich. It left many more broke and looking for the next gold rush.

A hundred years later, everything has changed and nothing has changed. The Iditarod race hasn't exactly made anyone rich, but it has left a few comfortably well off and famous. It has left more broke or broken hearted, their bank accounts drained, their dreams crushed.

Men, and an ever-increasing number of women, still take to the trail every year much as the gold seekers did. But they come now in pursuit of adventure, not gold. And strange though it may seem, the adventure of today sometimes means more to them than the gold meant to those poor, struggling seekers of fortune chasing a dream north through the wilderness and bitter cold just after the start of the 20th century.

The gold seekers, by and large, had a simple goal: money. The adventure seekers have a different and more complex goal. Most of them are searching for themselves, or at least that part of their being that sets them apart from their contemporaries, that part which is strong enough and smart enough and brave enough to do what few can do.

In the 37-year history of the Iditarod Trail Sled Dog Race, fewer than a thousand people have made it from the starting line in Anchorage to the finish line in Nome. More people than that had reached the top of Mount Everest, the world's tallest and deadliest mountain, by the end of the 20th century. By 2005, more than twice as many people had reached the summit of Everest as had managed to reach Nome by dog team in the Iditarod.

Climbing Everest is hard and dangerous. The high slopes of the 29,029-foot mountain are littered with the unrecoverable bodies of those who didn't make it back. The Iditarod, too, is dangerous, but it is not deadly. Many have been injured, but none – as yet – have died.

Still, running the Iditarod is arguably harder than climbing Everest. Not because of thin air; the trail never climbs higher than 3,200 feet. Not because of near-hurricane force winds, though such winds have sometimes battered mushers along the Bering Sea coast. Not even because of the cold, though the 45-to 50-degree-below-zero temperatures that regularly settle over the Alaska Interior are colder than those normally witnessed on Everest during the climbing season.

What makes the Iditarod so challenging are the dogs. Man's best friend can be a fickle, demanding, injury-prone beast. As five-time Iditarod champ Rick Swenson, the winningest musher in race history, once observed: "If all you had to do was put gas in them and go, anyone could do the Iditarod."

People like Swenson and his fellow champions – Lance Mackey, Jeff King, Martin Buser, Mitch Seavey – make Iditarod look so, so easy. These are mushers enjoying life behind teams of superbly trained and conditioned canine athletes. At the start on the streets of Anchorage, they jump on the runners of a dog sled, yell "Hike!" and away they go, the dogs charging merrily down the street. Anyone, it would appear, could do this.

David Aisenbrey, a kindly man from Montana Creek, a cluster of homes along the George Parks Highway north of Anchorage, knows better. Six times between 1984 and 1993, he started the Iditarod. Each year, he trained hard all winter with a team of huskies. Each year, he exhausted his savings on dog food and equipment. Each year, he came to Anchorage prepared as best he could to confront "The Last Great Race." He never had a prayer of winning. He wanted only to get to Nome with his dogs. He never made it.

The closest he ever got was Shaktoolik, a windswept village on a spit of sand tight against the Bering Sea. He had come 800 miles. There were only 200 miles of snow-covered tundra, sea ice and a couple patches of forest left between him and the finish, but he never got to see them. His dogs decided they'd had enough, and if the dogs won't go, the musher can't go.

"How hard is it?" asks Aisenbrey, now 77 years old and retired from mushing. "I think it's pretty hard. But I wish I was back there."

Even now, he cannot fully escape the Iditarod dream. He confesses that it was not easy to walk away. When Aisenbrey finally gave it up, he had to sell everything to get free – the dogs, the dog sleds, the gear, even the doghouses in the yard outside his home. He feared that if even a hint of his former life remained, he might be lured back.

In his dog days, Aisenbrey and his wife, Evelyn, lived in a 12-foot by 12-foot cabin. It was all they could afford given the gobbling sounds of sled dogs eating up their income. Since Aisenbrey left dogs, the couple has moved to a comfortable home near the community of Talkeetna. He now tinkers in a workshop the size of the house in which he used to live. He and Evelyn take vacations, something they could never afford to do before. The Iditarod, Aisenbrey admits, is a form of madness.

"When you get hooked on it," he said, "you do some stupid things, but I don't regret it."

Few do. The Iditarod might crush dreams and break hearts but it leaves all who enter feeling somehow different than their fellow man. For most who enter, the Iditarod is the biggest, grandest, craziest thing they will ever do.

The late Norman Vaughan, Antarctic explorer and Iditarod veteran, liked to extol these wannabees to "dream big and dare to fail." The stories that follow are of the people who took his advice.

That most of them failed, that most of them left their dreams dead along the Iditarod Trail, is not an indictment of their failures but a celebration of their courage. Jack London, a man of the Klondike, once observed that he would rather his spark burn out in a brilliant blaze than be stifled by dry-rot. "I would rather be a superb meteor, every atom of me in magnificent glow, than a sleepy and permanent planet. The function of man is to live, not just exist. I shall not waste my days trying to prolong them." That sentiment, often repeated but of undocumented origin, defines those with the courage to challenge life.

This book is about those who sought the brilliant blaze. This book is about those who stepped onto the Iditarod Trail to chase their dreams in the year 2010. As the title would indicate, it is mainly about those who tried and failed. But the book would not be complete without the stories of a couple whose dreams should have died, but somehow survived. Montana's Celeste Davis should have gone straight from the trail to a hospital, but she grabbed her badly broken nose with a gloved hand, wiggled it back into place in the middle of her smashed face, stemmed the bleeding that was painting the Dalzell Gorge red, and got back on the runners of her dog sled to mush another 750 miles or so to the Iditarod finish line.

And then there was philosopher Scott White from Washington state, whose dogs decided that 980 miles of trail was enough for them. At the Safety Roadhouse, only 20 miles from the finish, they quit pulling and bedded down. White couldn't get them to leave. There wasn't a dog in the team that wanted to lead the way to Nome. But White discovered that if he led, the dogs would follow. And so began a long march to reach Nome. The beginning to the end of his Iditarod was a throwback to the earliest days of sled dogs in Alaska when men were often at the front of the teams, but it did not end that way. Eventually, as most anyone who has walked a dog on a leash knows, the dogs decided that man-pace was too slow and passed their leader. White hopped the runners as his dog sled went by and rode to the finish.

His Iditarod dream might have ended up a little tarnished, but it was fulfilled. The coveted belt buckle given Iditarod finishers was his.

"This race is crazy," he said after. "I want to come back."

The "come back" theme resonates throughout these chapters: The come back from the brink, the come back from heartbreak, the come back time and again by those who should have quit. But one come back story bears telling first because it is a remarkable tale that spans both the despair and glory so exemplified by the Iditarod. It is the story of Lance Mackey and his Comeback Kennel.

Graveyard of Dreams

Dashed Hopes and Shattered Aspirations
Along Alaska's Iditarod Trail

1

Lance Mackey

Before there was four-time Iditarod Sled Dog Race champ Lance Mackey, there was a struggling Iditarod back-of-the-pack dog driver named Lance Mackey living in a shack on the Kenai Peninsula dreaming an impossible dream. No one – other than his wife Tonya – would have believed that Lance would ever achieve what he did in winning the Iditarod. His life since high school had, after all, been a train wreck.

He was married, divorced, the father of a young daughter, pursued for unpaid child support, delinquent on taxes, charged with theft and forgery and sorely disappointing his father – 1978 Iditarod champ Dick Mackey. Dick said he never gave up on Lance, but parents almost always say that. In Lance's case, you had to wonder just how close his father came.

But Lance was a hard worker. Skippers who hired him to work as crew on commercial fishing boats in the Bering Sea attested to that. Still, the trajectory of his life was arcing downward until Tonya re-entered the picture. They'd been classmates in elementary school in Big Lake then had gone their own ways. Tonya, originally Tonga, had her own crazy story. She was a single mother staying in Nenana with two daughters on that fateful day Lance hit her up for a ride down the road to Fairbanks. Lance's Nenana connection was half-brother Rick, whose Happy Dog Kennel is there at the wide spot in the George Parks Highway next to the big bridge over the Tanana River.

Lance and Tonya reconnected on the ride to town, married in 1997 and slowly changed their lives. The process started with a move to the Kenai Peninsula in 1998. Tonya had a relative living there, and Lance had a line on a possible job. Half-brother Rick was friends with 1985 Iditarod Rookie of the Year Tim Moerlein, whose wife ran a commercial salmon setnet site on a Cook Inlet beach. Though Moerlein had bailed out of the Iditarod years before, he maintained plenty of dog connections. Born and reared in Anchorage and educated at Dartmouth College, Moerlein is a smart guy. He understood early on it was senseless for him to dream of Iditarod victory.

Despite his athleticism and his days as a top cross-country skier, his size and weight were destined to prevent him from ever doing much better than his 11th place Iditarod finish as a rookie. A 6-foot, 3-inch guy was never going to beat Susan Butcher, then the Queen of the Iditarod Trail. Moerlein weighed 210 pounds. Butcher weighed 140. Right there, her team gained a 70-pound advantage, more than the weight of an extra dog in the sled. And that was just the start of it. Since a tall man needed a bigger sleeping bag, bigger clothing, bigger everything than a petite woman, the extra weight the team had to pull grew exponentially. Moerlein recognized he wasn't just in a battle with other mushers, but a fight with the realities of physics. He quit dog racing to focus his energies on building Moerlein

General Contracting into a successful business and helping wife, Kristina, with her commercial fishing operation. It was there he met Lance.

"Lance just sort of showed up at our setnet site one time," Tim said. "I didn't know him from Adam."

The Moerleins did, however, know the Mackey name. That was enough. They hired the skinny, long-haired musher wannabe and set him to work picking fish from the nets. Lance didn't look like much. Scrawny would be a kind description, but he worked hard.

"He didn't strike you as a guy that had any ambition or drive," Tim added, but that might have been because Lance had no great desire to be a commercial fisherman. Instead he had another dream, a crazy dream. He wanted to be a top Alaska dog musher. He wanted to follow in the footsteps of his dad, Dick, and brother, Rick, and win the Iditarod. He drafted a five-year plan to get there and laid it out to his wife.

No one but Tonya fully knows the steps he planned to follow in that five-year plan, but what is known is the fact that the Mackeys had no sled dog sponsors and no cash with which to start buying dogs. Home for the Mackeys and their children at the time was a cross between a shack and a tent on some bluff property overlooking a Cook Inlet beach. As the story goes, they were camped on property owned by an old family acquaintance.

"They were living raw," said Kenai friend Doug Ruzicka. The three Mackey daughters – one of Lance's and two of Tonya's – sometimes scavenged the beaches for flounder to eat. The family made regular visits to the local food bank. Lance would later, jokingly, refer to this period as the "Clampett" days, as in Jed Clampett of the old television series "The Beverly Hillbillies."

Given the reality of the situation, most people would not have been thinking about starting a dog team. But Lance is not most people. He marked the dawn of the new millennium by pulling together husky castoffs and rejects from the kennels of other Kenai mushers. Having grown up around his dad's kennel and having spent time at his brother's, Lance figured the one thing he knew was dogs.

But it didn't look that way in his first Iditarod race in 2001. The musher who could barely scrape together the $1,750 entry fee showed up at the start line in a rusting $300 Dodge truck towing a ratty dog trailer. He ended the race about where the best of ragtag mushers were expected to finish – 36th. Doug Swingley, a wealthy rancher from Montana, won that year, bringing his total Iditarod victories to four. Linwood Fiedler, a musher with a master's degree in behavioral studies, was second. Jeff King, a former champion sponsored by one of the nation's largest retailers of outdoor gear, was third.

Nobody even noticed skinny, dog hair-covered Lance in his tattered snowsuit back in the pack. He wasn't a smooth talker like former race veterinarian Sonny King, a budding contender who finished ninth. He wasn't the Next Great Hope like Rookie of the Year Jessie Royer who finished in 14th place. He wasn't even as good as Andy Moderow, a college kid from Anchorage who spent a season as the dog handler for former champ Martin Buser and then took Buser's second-string team to a top-20 finish. And Lance clearly was no Swingley.

The good news for Lance was that he didn't have much time after the race to dwell on what had gone wrong. Three days after finishing Iditarod, the musher was told the mind-rattling headaches that had plagued him during the race were due not to an abscessed tooth as doctors first thought, but were the symptoms of a cancerous tumor growing in his neck. Kenai Dr. James Zirul discovered it when he tried to drain the abscess. Anchorage surgeon William Fell told Lance it would have to be cut out.

The musher had neither money nor health insurance. Only weeks after the Iditarod ended, however, Fell and Zirul went ahead with the surgery anyway. The doctors were forced to cut lymph nodes, neck muscles, salivary glands and nerves from Mackey's neck to make sure all of the cancer was removed. Then to guard against the cancer's return, they ordered Mackey into 12 weeks of radiation treatment. The radiation zapped anything that might have been left of the cancer, but made a mess of Mackey's jaw-bone. He eventually had to have 10 teeth pulled. Sixteen weeks in a hyperbaric chamber followed to force oxygen into his skin to rebuild the red blood cells needed for his radiation-cooked cheek and jawbone to heal.

Gradually, he got better, but there was permanent damage. He was unable to lift his right arm over his head. He had no salivary glands and was forced to carry a water bottle everywhere to keep his throat moist so he could breath. His left pointer finger was numb and pretty much useless. He eventually told a doctor to cut it off because all it was good for was getting in the way.

He was no longer just broke, either. Now he found himself buried under a Mount McKinley-size pile of debt from medical bills. Strangely enough, that turned out to be a blessing. Because of his health condition and lack of money, he qualified for federal Medicaid and disability insurance. These aren't exactly things anyone brags about in Alaska where government "socialism" is a four-letter word, but America's social safety net saved Lance.

Fell, Zirul and other doctors, meanwhile, began donating money to sponsor Mackey's Comeback Kennel. They thought the musher's recovery would be aided by the continued pursuit of his Iditarod dream. Tonya got a job waiting tables in Kenai to help with finances, and Team Mackey lurched forward.

Lance managed to start the 2002 race with a feeding tube still in his stomach to keep him nourished while undergoing chemotherapy. But he was in no shape to do the race, something he realized before he got halfway to Nome. He quit at the Ophir checkpoint: number 34th. He won recognition for displaying the tenacity to try, and most mushers would have been happy with that small victory.

Some wondered if his Iditarod experiment was over. Lance skipped the Iditarod in 2003, but did score a victory in the Knik 200 Sled Dog Race that year and cleaned up in the race's "Ugliest Truck" competition, too. The dog race victory was a bit of a surprise, the ugly truck victory a slam-dunk. Lance was still king of the clunkers. The idea of "Lance Mackey, Iditarod champion" was, however, unimaginable. When the words "Mackey" and "Iditarod champion" appeared in the same sentence, the subject was never Lance but half-brother Rick, the 1983 champ, and a top-10 contender through the '90s and into the new century.

None of that changed as the Comeback Kennel rolled into 2004: year four of the five-year plan. Lance did score a best ever Iditarod finish and won $5,300, but he was hardly noticed back in 24th place.

In year five of the plan, Lance and Tonya shifted their

base of operations from Kasilof to Fairbanks to find better snow, and Lance moved on to the 1,000-mile Yukon Quest International Sled Dog Race from Fairbanks to Whitehorse, Yukon Territory, Canada. His tough dogs, he believed, had a better chance in a race thought to be more about endurance than speed. Weeks before Iditarod, Lance won his first Quest, then headed south to run Iditarod.

No one had ever known any success in running the two biggest races back-to-back. No one expected Lance to change that, but he did. He was seventh in Iditarod 2005. Everyone in the small world of long-distance, sled dog racing took notice, and then wrote it off as a fluke. A 10th-place finish the next year after a second Quest victory convinced the critics they had been right. No Quest victor could ever hope to win Iditarod, they said. To win the Iditarod, a musher had to focus on that race and that race alone.

A year later, Lance proved them wrong. In 2007, he rocked the mushing world by winning the two grueling races back-to-back with essentially the same dogs. This wasn't some sort of four-minute-mile feat everyone could see coming long ahead of time. This was an achievement so far in front of the curve that it preceded any suggestion it might be feasible. And the next year, Lance did it again.

If ever there was a character to fuel the dreams of Iditarod wannabes, here he was. Lance didn't have the academic pedigree of Swiss-educated, four-time champ Buser from Big Lake, or the financial backing of businessman King from Denali Park, another four-time winner. Lance didn't have the connections of the late, four-time champ Butcher, born in Cambridge, Massachusetts to a Harvard-educated father who ran a multi-million dollar business while serving on the boards of influential biotech and bio-medical companies, or the experience of five-time champ Swenson from Two Rivers.

Lance was the living, breathing illustration that almost anyone could win the Iditarod. Or at least anyone could if they had the magic of Lance Mackey. He was the Iditarod magician, the guy who won though no one could quite figure out how. Others talked a better game. Others could make claim to owning faster dogs. A lot of others looked tougher. And yet, there at the finish line in Nome, was Lance, the man with the five-year plan and a grin on his face looking back at the others who could only wonder how he got there first.

Someone called him the "everyman musher," and he was, but he wasn't. His victories weren't representative of the possibility anyone could win the Iditarod; they were representative of the idea a plan well worked by a phe-nom could dominate the Iditarod. The lesson wasn't "if Lance can do it; anyone can do it;" the lesson was that it's hard to beat a musher who has the body of a sled dog jockey, a special gift for working with canines and a focus spawned of a near-death experience. Lance emerged from his battle with cancer a different man. He was unique. He was a one-of. The "everyman musher" was really Linwood Fiedler, DeeDee Jonrowe, Eep Anderson, Herbie Nayokpuk, Sonny Lindner, Paul Gebhardt, Ramy Brooks, Joe Garnie, Duane "Dewey" Halverson and all the others who'd come oh-so-close to Iditarod victory over the years, and yet never won.

Halverson might be the most notable among them. He was the invisible musher, the first loser in 1985 when the Iditarod vaulted from being a somewhat esoteric event in frozen Alaska to a global story. Libby Riddles, Halverson's ex-girlfriend, was the reason why. Riddles was the first woman to win the "grueling Iditarod." But it wasn't just that she was the first woman champion. It was how she won – urging her team through a Bering coast blizzard that intimidated her male competitors in the front of the pack. It was how she looked – tall, blonde, attractive – and the way she lived. The former Minnesotan had made a home for herself in the tiny, primitive Northwest Alaska coastal village of Teller with Native Alaska sled dog guru Joe Garnie. The media made much of her story. Riddles was even featured in Vogue magazine, and she looked like she belonged there.

Riddles became an international celebrity. Halverson became one of the faceless men in the budding slogan – "Alaska, where men are men and women win the Iditarod!" It was a sad fate for a man who sacrificed mightily to contend in the Iditarod of the '80s. He raised and then lost a fortune running Iditarod. He went through wives and girlfriends the way others went through dog handlers, though this might have had something to do with the wives and girlfriends sometimes being courted as potential dog handlers. He was a man who saw some mighty good highs and some pretty low lows. He insists now that the rumor is untrue that he and then girlfriend Chris O'Gar were at one time living on ground turkey they bought to feed their dogs.

"The only dog food we ever ate was this lamb you could buy with ash on it," Halverson said. "You could cut that ash off. That meat was edible."

Suffice it to say, Halverson's dogs sometimes ate at least as well as he, his girlfriends or his wives. Halverson went through four of the latter. Dogs ate up his life, his money and all of his attention. Always an operator, he never seemed to run short of marketing ideas, but he could never come up with new ones fast enough to keep up with the way he was spending money on dogs, dog food and gear in hopes of winning just one, stupid Iditarod race. He might have been, it should be noted, the first musher to offer sponsors a ride with his team through the streets of Anchorage on the first day of the Iditarod race. It was an incentive to donate more money to the Halverson cause. His rider idea eventually morphed into the Idita-rider auction, which with the help of a public relations push from State of Alaska tourism, now generates substantial revenue for the Iditarod Trail Committee. It didn't generate enough money to keep Halverson afloat.

"By the end of it, I was just owing everybody money," he said. "My eyes were always bigger than my ability to pay for things. I once compared myself to a junkie, but that would have been a lot cheaper and easier. Taking care of those dogs is just bullshit. Just think, if I'd put that kind of work into a business, I'd be a jillionaire."

A whole lot of people involved with Iditarod – veterans,

rookies and those who attempted the race only to come up short – are familiar with this tune. The Iditarod exerts a powerful pull. Nancy Yoshida, a 59-year-old occupational therapist from North Dakota, crashed out of the 2009 race then spent days in the Alaska Range looking for a lost dog. It was a miserable experience. Yet afterward, she immediately started training to be back in 2010. She paid the now $4,600 entry fee – an amount Mackey would never have been able to afford in his rookie year – but had to drop out before the race because of problems back home. That didn't derail her Iditarod pursuit, however. At last report, she was shopping for land in northern Minnesota to make dog training easier so she can come back to Iditarod in 2011 or 2012. "I'm so happy my husband puts up with this," she said. Her husband is a physician specializing in ear, nose and throat. He has the money to help pay the bills for her sled dog addiction.

"If you have never stood behind a dog team," she says on the website for her Reach for the Sky Kennel, "I would suggest that you try it if the opportunity arises. Beware though, as it is habit forming."

Halverson, too, used to encourage people to get on the runners back in the day. "I was a pusher," he said. The memories of his own habit are still hard to shake. "I'd love to get behind a dog team again," he admitted, "maybe train or take care of somebody's yearlings for a year and run them and give them back. It was a great adventure. But the reality is I'm 58 now. What's the point of beating my head against the wall? Swenson, who is obviously a competent dog driver with a good system, advised me it might be a good idea to get out early instead of falling farther and farther back every year."

Halverson took the advice. He got out. In his own way, he won against the Iditarod. He got a life. He found other interests. "Some of these people are not multi-faceted people," Halverson said. "It's hard for them to go outside of that box. After one race, I remember, I talked to Rick Mackey and some other guys and said, 'Hey, let's go to Mexico and SCUBA dive, relax, have some fun.' They looked at me like, 'What? Leave the dogs?'"

Top to bottom, there remains this commonality to the Iditarod today. Mushers end up married to their dogs. They live, breathe and smell dogs. When they dream, they dream Iditarod. All that separates the contenders from the back-of-packers, really, is the vision of what comes at the end of the dream. For some, the only measure of success is victory. For others, the victory is simply to finish. Everyone would like to be like Lance, but plenty would be happy to be John Schultz, the first winner of the red lantern. The red lantern is the prize given to the last musher to arrive in Nome. It took Schultz more than a month to get from Anchorage to the Iditarod finish line in 1973, but he got there. He beat the Iditarod the way Lance Mackey beat cancer, not by going fast but by gutting it out.

2

The Dream

To understand the people who ran Iditarod 2010 and most of those who came before, you must first understand the Iditarod is more than just a race. It is an addictive fantasy about a partnership with man's best friend wrapped in the mythology of the north. It is a step back into time, a chance to live a piece of history.

Jack London – the author of *The Call of the Wild*, *White Fang* and a whole bunch of short stories about gold rush days in the north – might have died in 1916, but a part of him lives on along this trail. The same can be said for Robert Service, "The Bard of the Yukon," and television's "Sergeant Preston of the Yukon," the fictional representative of the Royal Canadian Mounted Police who first materialized in a radio serial along with lead dog "King" in 1938 and then mushed into the beginnings of TV in the 1950s.

Fictional characters from another time – London's Malemute Kid and Service's Sam McGee – provide the back story for the real-life Iditarod characters. There are the still-living – "Yukon Fox" Emmit Peters and Skwentna mainstay Joe Delia. There are the dead – Herbie Nayokpuk, the Shishmaref Cannonball; Joe Redington, Sr., the Father of the Iditarod; and Susan Butcher whose dominance drove home the slogan, "Alaska – Where men are men and women win the Iditarod."

Delia, strangely enough, never ran the Iditarod, but he somehow ended up in the thick of the cast of Iditarod characters. His daughter, Christine, won the Junior Iditarod in 1981, and Joe and wife Norma's old home in Skwentna on the threshold between Anchorage and the Alaska Range has forever been the Iditarod checkpoint. Years back, the Delia's moved next door and donated their two-story log house to the race. The stories that have been told around the tables inside are legend.

Elfin Iditarod founder Redington, who started the Iditarod madness in 1973, used to sit there and weave tales about his days hauling freight in Alaska with dog teams. If there was something that needed to be towed out of some inaccessible corner of the Alaska Range, Redington and his dogs somehow managed to get to it and bring it back. They hauled airplanes. They hauled diesel generators. They hauled loads that would in these days be unbelievable.

Redington thought dogs could do just about anything. He took some of them to the top of 20,320-foot Mount McKinley in 1979 along with understudy Butcher, guide Brian Okonek, the legendary late mountaineer Ray "Pirate" Genet, and photographer Rob Stapleton. Genet was destined to die descending from the top of Mount Everest only months later. Butcher would, meanwhile, move on to a tiny cabin in Manley in the Interior where she and a gang of dogs who were her best friends would begin to lay the groundwork for an Iditarod dynasty. Before her premature death from cancer in 2006, she would go on to win four Iditarods.

Redington never did win the race he started. The best he ever did was fifth, the first time in 1975 at the age of 58, the last time in 1988 at the age of 71. Redington died of cancer in 1999, but his presence looms over the race still. Back in the day, he would sit in the Delia cabin and tell stories that held other mushers and race fans enthralled. Delia, meanwhile, would get them to laughing until they had to hold their sides. Delia, the other Joe, was the consummate Alaska Bush rat. He is aging now and battling one health problem after another, but there was a time when he owned the wild places and was wildly admired for it. You could have dropped him out of an airplane in the middle of nowhere with nothing but a pocketknife, and in short time, he would have built a cabin, gathered enough wood and food for the winter, set himself up in business running a trap line, and maybe even started building his own electric generator so he could have light to read the books he would be writing in his free time.

That is the Joe D. known to most every musher who has traveled the trail since the beginning of the Iditarod. But there was one time a Cheechako Joe D. He came to life in the stories told by the strong but gentle, self-effacing Alaska pioneer who built the Iditarod checkpoint in Skwentna, and that Cheechako Joe D. was one hilarious greenhorn, a stumbler and a bumbler with whom the greenest of Iditarod rookies could identify.

Cheeckako Joe, a son of the South, tried to get to Alaska by paddling an Army surplus raft up the Green River in Seattle after the Second World War. He thought he was riding the current to sea. Someone had to point out to him he was riding an incoming tide inland in the direction of Oregon. Delia eventually took a freighter north to

Ketchikan.

Once on the ground in the 49th state, he migrated toward Big Lake, now a popular recreation area north of Anchorage. There was a whole lot of nothing there when Delia arrived. He built his first cabin with his own hands. The cracks between the logs were big enough for squirrels to crawl through. He covered the roof with thatch because he didn't have any idea what else to cover it with. The thatch leaked. Every time it snowed that winter, and it snowed a lot in those days, the heat of the cabin melted the snow on the roof, and Delia got a shower.

Half starved by the middle of winter, he was lucky to have a moose walk into his yard. He grabbed his gun and shot it. It walked a few steps and wedged itself upright between a pair of trees. Delia wasn't quite sure what to do next. While he was trying to figure out how to get the moose out of the tree, it froze in place. For much of the rest of the winter, he said, he was trekking out to the frozen moose to chop out chunks of meat to throw in his cooking pot. Since the moose had never been skinned, he often ended up with almost as much moose hair as meat in the pot, but he survived, and he thrived, and eventually he moved north to Skwentna, which is what is now called a "census-designated place," which is to say there really is no there there.

A well-established checkpoint for the modern Iditarod dog race, Skwentna wasn't even on the original trail. The Iditarod ran past a dog barn and rest stop called the Skwentna roadhouse almost 10 miles to the west, and then headed almost due south to Susitna Station, the old riverboat stop, on the Susitna River. That historic stretch of the Iditarod Trail is today almost abandoned.

The trail changed as times changed. The airplane came to Skwentna. The military, intent on protecting Alaska from a resurgent Soviet Union, set up a base nearby. A community coalesced around an airstrip. Lodges began to develop in the area. The snowmachine arrived to connect them. Traffic began to move away from the trail onto the rivers. Only the vision of Redington kept the old trail alive. For years he insisted on sticking to the traditional route.

There is no doubt this made the race harder. The regular snowmachine traffic to Skwentna was already moving along the wide-open Susitna, Yentna and Skwentna rivers. The trail through the woods had to be put in specifically for the Iditarod race. It was a winding route that ran up and down hills and oft times forced teams to plod through deep snow. In 1992, the team of rookie William Orazietti, a Maytag repairman from Sault St. Marie, Ontario, Canada, floundered on this stretch of trail. It took him a couple days to reach Skwentna, where he promptly dropped out of the race.

That sort of thing just doesn't happen anymore. The race now follows the snowmachine routes along the rivers. Even Old Joe eventually had to concede that was the sensible thing to do. Given the hard-packed snowmachine trail that runs up the Yentna and Skwentna rivers, it is rare for anyone to scratch on the first leg of The Last Great Race to Skwenta unless they are suffering badly from something like author Gary Paulsen's hemorrhoids, or have hopelessly sick dogs. There were no such dogs in 2010, and so the race sped through Skwentna into the swamps to the south and west on its way up into the Shell Hills and on toward Finger Lake.

Usually this, too, is a pretty easy stretch of trail. Usually.

3

Anchorage to Skwentna

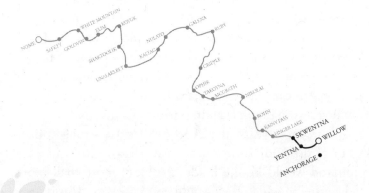

From the urban comfort of Anchorage, the 1,000-mile Iditarod Trail Sled Dog Race looks tantalizingly simple. Rookie mushers arriving in the city are to be excused if they fail to recognize the size of the challenge they are about to face. By dint of the requirements of race rules, they come to the start having already spent hundreds of miles on the runners of a dog sled in qualifying races. It is only natural that most think themselves seasoned and ready. These thoughts are only reinforced by what is seen from the Alaska roadside.

First there is the familiarity of Alaska's largest city with its hum and bustle and comforting civility. If not for the Chugach Mountains looming tight and wild against Anchorage's eastern edge, this could be Anywhere, America with its roadside strips of development defined by shopping malls and the ubiquitous, continent-roaming fast food restaurants and discount store franchises. McDonalds? Check, bunches of them. Wal-Mart? Likewise. Starbucks? Yes. Taco Bell, Home Depot, Lowes, T.G.I. Friday's, Ace Hardware and on and on ad infinitum.

The only mushers likely to find themselves uncomfortable in the city are those coming from rural Alaska or some desolate part of the American West, and there aren't many mushers from either these days. The modern Iditarod is an expensive proposition that attracts a small group of professionals competing for the $50,000 top prize and a mob of college-educated adventurers with money, connections or a willingness to sacrifice all in pursuit of a dream.

As in most years, the 2010 field had a strong contingent of these Idit-a-dreamers. Many had yet to realize the Iditarod would be the hardest, coldest, most challenging adventure in which they would ever take part. This is to be understood. It is impossible to explain to the uninitiated the debilitating reality of sleep deprivation and existence at 40 and 50 degrees below zero. At these sorts of temperatures, it is difficult for people to care for themselves let alone care for a pack of dogs or repair broken equipment. Some would conclude they could not endure. Most would hang on.

When the Iditarod is described as an ultra-endurance event, this is what the word means. You endure. You walk up and down the trail for three hours at 45 degrees below zero to keep from freezing to death while your dogs get needed rest curled up on piles of straw. You shake your fingers in your oversize mitts to keep them warm, feel the frost forming on the fur ruff of the parka hood protecting your face from the icy fangs of the sub-arctic cold, and hope for better in the morning, hope that in the feeble sunshine of the new day in the far north there might be a few degrees of life-supporting heat.

There is no thought of this, of course, at the beginning of Iditarod, where the race isn't even a race. At the start the city is warm and friendly, and the Iditarod is nothing more than a parade down Fourth Avenue in Anchorage onto city streets and bike trails. This is a show for the cameras and the fans, an Iditarod spectacle carried live on local television for the thousands who chose not to join the mobs on the streets paying witness.

Once it was different. Once mushers raced 25 miles from downtown to the suburb of Eagle River, scrambled to load dogs and gear into dog trucks, raced another 30 miles out the Glenn and George Parks highways to follow the Knik-Goose Bay Road to the hometown of Iditarod-founder Joe Redington, hurried to unload and unpack, and then raced off on the trail to Nome.

This eventually ended because of all the dog teams that fried on the Eagle River run. They didn't literally fry, but they came close. Veterinarians kept ice baths ready at the Eagle River checkpoint for the emergency treatment of overheated dogs. Hyperthermia hasn't killed many, but it has taken a lot of top teams out of contention. Dogs physically weakened by heat exhaustion at the start of the race couldn't get back into condition to compete until the eventual winners were well beyond them on the trail.

When it was suggested the Anchorage race start be abandoned in favor of an Anchorage race celebration, no mushers objected. The big hoopla in Alaska's largest city thus became a big show, though to this day it maintains the appearance of a race. Teams still leave Fifth Avenue at two-minute intervals. There is still a countdown before each team is told "Go!" But it's ceremonial.

Instead of racing to Eagle River, the teams take paying Idita-riders on an 11-mile jaunt along city streets and bike trails to a park called the Campbell Tract. The whole exercise takes up a morning and part of an afternoon. Then all the competitors and their teams pack up and go off to get a good night's sleep while the Idita-riders go home with their Idit-a-dreams.

Loyola University grad Pat Moon was one of those Idita-riders in 2006. He went back to Illinois with a monster of a dream. He envisioned that one day he would do more than just ride in an Iditarod dog sled. He foresaw himself directing a dog team all the way to Nome. He spent the next four years of his life in pursuit of this dream.

When Iditarod 2010 began in downtown Anchorage, Moon was on the runners of his own dog sled hauling Idita-rider Claudia Nowark from Traverse City, Michigan, through the corridor of store fronts and high rises, past the apartments along Cordova Avenue and down the big hill that leads to the trails in the city's brushy, tree-filled Chester Creek greenbelt. Nowark's little adventure would be over in about an hour. Moon's big adventure would begin nearly 24 hours later.

The modern Iditarod competition starts for real on a Sunday, 75 miles to the north of Anchorage at a wide spot on the George Parks Highway called Willow. There is an airstrip there, a few businesses scattered about, and a trail heading west and then south through the spruce/birch forests and across frozen lakes to the Susitna River. This trail is well groomed with only one big hill to descend. And, once on the river, mushers face easy sledding for the first

30 miles downstream on the snow-covered ice and then upstream on the frozen Yentna River into the first Iditarod checkpoint of Yentna Station. From there, the race generally moves flawlessly on to the second checkpoint at Skwentna.

It used to be different. There was a time when the race followed the historic Iditarod route from the tiny, old Cook Inlet port of Knik to a deserted riverboat landing at Susitna Station and then went overland through the forest west of the Yentna River to Skwentna. Knik, however, was abandoned as a race checkpoint as Wasilla oozed west in suburban sprawl, and the historic Iditarod Trail was sacrificed in the name of convenience. A snowmachine highway these days follows the river ice from near Willow to Skwentna, and the mushers are happy to follow it. Well-packed and heavily traveled, it speeds the race north with an ease unknown in the Iditarod's early years.

By the time rookie mushers reach Skwentna, they may start to think the race is overrated. Sure, it's 1,000 miles long, but it appears doable. Sure, there are better dog teams at the front of the pack, but a tenth of the way into the race they don't look that much better. In 2010, all 71 Iditarod teams arrived at Skwentna within eight hours of the race start.

Round-faced, 33-year-old Moon was among them. A teenage victim of an autoimmune disease and now battling non-Hodgkin lymphoma, he had hopes of using his Iditarod experience to further a budding career as an inspirational speaker. His theme: "Leading from the rear." He made Skwentna without a problem. So, too, did petite Kathleen Frederick, a temporarily out-of-work 58-year-old attorney originally from Bryn Mar, Pennsylvania. Joining them was a cosmopolitan cast of characters from across the continent:

Goateed Emil Churchin, 42, a poet from Ohio who found the best-paying job he'd ever known screening digital images in the oil fields of Alaska's North Slope only to blow all his money on an Iditarod dream. Near jockey-size Scotsman John Stewart, 24, who'd grown up in a mushing family in the British Isles. East coast philosophy student turned West Coast businessman Scott White, 45, who'd nearly frozen his fingers off in his first, aborted attempt at the Iditarod in 2007. And, former model Zoya DeNure who spent more than a decade walking runways around the globe before falling in love with dogs and Alaska woodsman John Schandelmeier, who helped feed her dogged addiction. Now a 33-year-old mother, DeNure entered her second Iditarod thinking she might be able to compete for position despite having just weaned a baby girl.

All joined a field of former Iditarod champions in the hunt for another victory, proven veterans thinking this could be their year, the latest collection of new hopefuls, and the seasoned, trail-savvy mushers who knew they didn't have a chance of winning, but who couldn't stay away. Jolly Karen Ramstead, a breeder of Siberian husky show dogs from Perryvalle, Alberta, Canada was entered in her ninth Iditarod. Four of her previous eight races ended short of the finish line in Nome. Her team's best finish was 56th, which was considered quite good for someone who chose to run a team of big, purebred dogs many mushers jokingly referred to as Slow-berians.

She wasn't, however, the only Slow-berian driver in the race. The breed still has its fans. Blake Freking from Finland, Minnesota was back with a team of purebred Siberians, too. He'd set a record for the breed in 2008 when he reached the Nome finish line in just under 11 days, 22 hours. He was 51st that year. Forty-five year-old Ramstead was hoping to beat the 36-year-old Freking to the finish in 2010. Ramstead and Freking were joined on the trail by Siberian fan Hank Debruin from Haliburton, Ontario, Canada. Debruin runs Winterdance Dogsled Tours on the edge of Canada's Algonquin Provincial Park. The 47-year-old had been dreaming about the Iditarod for most of his life. A friendly, bearded man, he was more about the romance of the Iditarod than the race.

Freking and Ramstead knew what they were getting into when they started north on the Iditarod Trail. Debruin and his dogs, like most rookies and their dogs, could only guess. And, if by Skwentna the race didn't seem all that tough, it is understandable. They had only arrived at the doorstep of the Alaska wilds. They would not find out how difficult the Iditarod can be until they crossed the threshold.

Most of the rookies happily took their first long break of the race on the snow-covered ice below the bluff where sits the log home of Joe and Norma Delia. Race contenders and some old hands familiar with the buzz of Skwentna paused only long enough to grab straw and food for the dogs before heading on along the trail to camp. The checkpoint was too close to the city for them. The skies overhead would roar with small planes on Monday as tourists flew in from around the world to see actual mushers and actual teams on the actual trail.

Skwentna itself isn't much – an airstrip, the Delia's cabin on the bluff above the river next to the post office, the Skwentna Roadhouse back in the woods, a scattering of homes hidden in the forest surrounding the airport, a school now abandoned for lack of students – but it comes alive for Iditarod. The graying residents from up and down river flood in to help staff the checkpoint at the Delia's. The airport grows busy with visitors.

During the 2010 race, as in years past, tourists stumbled through the dog lot down on the river where the dogs tried to rest on their piles of straw. They stuck cameras in the faces of everyone and everything. They crowded the checkpoint at the Delia's cabin and made most of the mushers there yearn for the wilderness ahead. For the few dog drivers who might have wanted to linger, the people were incentive enough to leave.

Ahead waited the true wilds that would test mushers and dogs, and all of the mushers yearned to embrace the challenge. Most of them remained convinced they were still comfortably in the game. Some years this self-deception can persist all the way to Finger Lake at the foot of the Alaska Range. In 2010, though, the race was going to end early for at least one musher as it moved into the Shell Hills. Mother Nature, as she is sometimes wont to do, was about to double down on the weather, and a normally easy trail was about to turn race-ending difficult.

4

Kirk Barnum

A week before the start of Iditarod 2010, the trail through the waist-deep snow covering the huge, open muskegs and narrow patches of forest on the benches for 30 miles between Skwentna and the checkpoint at Finger Lake was a horizontal luge run – a sled dog and snowmachine freeway in the bottom of a ditch banked by two-foot high walls.

Then Mother Nature tossed a curve ball. Snow started falling heavily. Wind blew it sideways across the muskegs. The ditch that was the trail began to fill. In some places, the trail disappeared. In other places, the ditch filled only part way. It was hard to say which was worse. The blown-in trail was sometimes hard to find. The partially filled-in trail could be found, but teams and mushers had to fight their way through it. Dog sleds tilted on their sides as one sled runner dived down into the ditch and the other hung up on hard, drifted, wind-packed snow.

These conditions might be seen as normal in a race hallmarked by its man-against-nature theme, but they would prove enough to defeat Montana forester Kirk Barnum. The 41-year-old Barnum, a sometimes fly-fishing guide who grew up in Northern California before moving east to the true West, is a thoughtful man. He entered the 2010 race not so much with a dream as with a plan for a dream born a full decade earlier:

Pull together a kennel of genetically blessed long-distance runners. Raise them up into one big, happy, hard-working family. Train them until they can run almost forever. Take them up the Iditarod Trail on a sled dog training run in 2008. And then return to race in 2010, make a mark, get some big-name sponsors and go professional.

It was not a bad plan. Former Iditarod champ Dean Osmar from Clam Gulch, Alaska, followed a similar strategy in the 1980s. He ran his rookie race in 1982 and finished 13 in a field of 46. That would be equivalent to about a 25th place finish in the larger, more competitive fields hitting the Iditarod trail in the 2000s. Osmar skipped the 1983 race to train and came back in 1984 to win.

Barnum's rookie run in 2008 wasn't quite as impressive. Barnum was 67th among 76 finishers. Still his finishing time of 13 days, 10 hours and 19 minutes was only 18 hours slower than Osmar's winning time. And Barnum didn't really expect to challenge for the championship in 2010. He hoped only to move into the upper cadre of Iditarod mushers against which he might challenge for victory in 2011.

Another musher with a background similar to Barnum's had done this, too. Barnum was trained in forestry; four-time Iditarod champ Martin Buser had been trained in horticulture. Buser put his scientific background to good use to grow his Happy Trails Kennel into one of the best in Alaska. Barnum hoped to duplicate the feat in Montana, but he needed money. He hoped that in 2010 he could show enough to encourage sponsors to back him in the years ahead, as Buser had done.

And Barnum should have done well. He had veteran dogs. He trained hard. And he fit the mold for the prototypical musher of the 21st century: lean, small-boned, almost jockey-like and Bush savvy.

A forester for 20 years, Barnum spent his time in the woods cruising the timber of the West to size up trees for lumber companies. When he wasn't doing that, he was at the oars of a drift boat guiding anglers or on the runners of a dog sled or plotting a future with dogs.

His Iditarod dreams went way back. He started running dogs in 1995 in California. By 1999, his sled dog addiction fully formed, he moved to Montana to become one with his canines. Soon he had a kennel of about 50 huskies. He'd raised most of them himself. They were, he said, good dogs, strong dogs. He had faith in them. He liked them, and he enjoyed riding behind them.

He came into Iditarod 2010 thinking an 11-day race imminently doable. With a little luck, he figured, he'd do even better and finish in the top 20. Early on, Barnum's race looked better than good. He headed out from Skwentna into the swamps less than an hour behind three-time and defending Iditarod champ Lance Mackey from Fairbanks. Four-time champ and perennial contender Jeff King from Denali Park was little more than half an hour in front.

"When we left Skwentna," Barnum said, "there was a rooster tail (of snow) behind me and a smile on my face."

That was almost enough to set a musher to contemplating the mother of all Iditarod dreams, the dangerous dream that one can be a contender, the dream for which Iditarod veteran Eric Rogers was paying the price. Just three days before that smile crossed Barnum's face leaving Skwentna, the following note appeared on the web page maintained by Rogers at rnorthbounddogs.com: "Sorry to have been so quiet. Our house is in active foreclosure with the sale at auction set for May 20th (2010). We've been pretty busy looking for work, alternative ways to make money (sponsorships, etc.) and training the dogs hoping for a miracle so I could run this year's Iditarod. If you know of a cheap place to rent in Alaska where I can keep a dog team with power and running water, please let me know. Kind thoughts and prayers are always appreciated."

Rogers is no wild-eyed young man. He is 61 years old and holds a doctorate in theoretical particle physics from the University of Washington. Before the Iditarod took over his life, he was a geophysicist for Shell Oil. He took a buyout in 1992 and moved to Anchorage because, he confessed, he'd been in love with the idea of Alaska since he'd read Jack London and watched Sgt. Preston as a kid.

Like many addicts, he managed to live a normal life even as his addiction was worsening. First for Rogers, as for Barnum, there was one dog and then a few dogs and then a whole bunch of dogs. Rogers, like Barnum, then started racing. Rogers, like Barnum, eventually started thinking he could do better. Rogers, like Barnum, decided his goal in life was to be a professional musher. It didn't happen. After two Iditarods, his dream was on the ropes. He was strapped for cash and wondering what to do next.

Blame for this in Rogers's case can probably be placed on Iditarod founder Joe Redington Sr., who didn't run his first race until he was 57 years old and then stayed competitive into his 70s. He was fifth in the 1988 Iditarod at the age of 71. He was ninth the next year. He made the impossible seem possible. Redington's performances – not to mention the antics of dog driver and showman Norman Vaughan – fueled the dreams of more than a few senior citizens. But there are even fewer Joe Redingtons and Norman Vaughans than there are Doug Swingleys, and there aren't many Swingleys. This little bit of reality isn't, however, enough, to stop the dreamers.

Barnum didn't yet see himself in the class of his Montana neighbor and four-time Iditarod champ Swingley, but he could see himself getting there. It was an easy thing to envision when he left Skwentna with a foot on the brake to keep the dogs from running too hard and the snow torn up by that brake flying up behind like a rooster-tail chasing a high-powered speedboat. Problem was that this boat was headed for the rocks. Disaster came via a cascade of little problems on the trail to Finger Lake.

Fifteen miles out of the Skwentna checkpoint, a little more than 100 miles into the 1,000-mile race to Nome, one of Barnum's dogs started to falter. The musher stopped to check on her. She clearly didn't appear up to running with the team anymore. Barnum decided he'd best haul her to Finger Lake and leave her with the veterinarians and dog handlers there.

Had the trail been hard-packed and firm, this likely would not have been a problem. Barnum and the rest of his team might barely have noticed another 50 pounds in the sled, or how the weight of the dog on top of the other gear made the sled top-heavy and tippy. But the trail was no longer hard-packed and firm. It was full of fresh snow that dragged at the sled and tried to tip it onto its side.

"It slowed me down to about three miles per hour," Barnum said.

His team went from running the pace of Iditarod leaders to less than the pace of the slowest Iditarod rookies and campers. Team after team began passing him, and some of them brought new problems. Back-of-the-pack teams do not operate with the same precision as those at the front. Three times, Barnum said, he found his team tangled up with other dog teams when they tried to pass. Straightening things out took time he didn't have to spare.

"It got worse and worse," he said, "and that was hard on my morale."

As Barnum's attitude soured, so did that of his team. This is one of the things that makes the Iditarod so hard. Dogs are emotion-sensing creatures prone to feast on the mood of the person in charge for better or for worse. In Barnum's case it was a lot to the worse.

Much of the race passed him by on the snow-filled, windswept trail from Skwentna to Finger. The 33rd team into Skwentna – in front of both King and eventual race-winner Mackey – Barnum's dogs found themselves 67th among 71 by Finger Lake with a broken man riding behind them. Barnum had given up.

"I've been to Nome," he said. "I've got my (finisher's) belt buckle."

He could find no good reason to press on, and his team knew it. You could see it in their eyes as they rested near the WeatherPORTs scattered across the snow-covered ice downhill from the world-class Winterlake Lodge at Finger. Barnum strolled up the snowmachine packed trail to the kitchen door and went inside. It was warm with the smell of fresh bread and spiced meats. Kirsten Dixon, the co-owner of the lodge and an internationally recognized chef, was in residence.

These are the sorts of things that can lift a man's flagging spirits along the trail, but not for Barnum. He had reached that point a musher sometimes reaches where there are no good things to be found. His fate, he said, belonged to a 10-year-old lead dog he never expected to go all the way to Nome, and "my other lead dog has chronic wrist problems." He didn't know what he'd do if he had to drop the old dog due to fatigue, a good possibility, or the younger dog due to a wrist gone from uncomfortable to painful, another good possibility.

"I think I could make it to Nome," he said, "but it wouldn't be pretty. It sucks. So I'm gonna scoot on up to Rainy Pass and wait for an airplane."

He would have called it quits at Finger, but for a shortage of dog food and the snowy weather that kept airplanes grounded. He was afraid his dogs might go hungry if he decided to stay, so he was taking most of the team and pushing on to the next checkpoint with rations waiting. He needed to find something positive to grasp, he knew, but all around him were the negatives.

"I wanted to make a career of this," he said, "but you need sponsors... You need to be able to give everything to dog mushing...they'll give a NASCAR driver a million dollars."

Yes, they will. An Iditarod dog musher, on the other hand, is lucky to get a pair of winter boots and a sled, but in some ways that's the least of it. "It's more than a money thing," Barnum said. "It's five years of my life. It's what you put up with to be a kennel owner."

And yet mushers keep coming back again and again. Twenty-seven years before Barnum's dream floundered in the snow on the way to Finger Lake, Montanan Terry

Adkins saw his come to a far more inglorious end in the Topkok Hills outside of Nome. Adkins was running with the race leaders until his team quit. He camped with them for a day. It didn't help. They still refused to continue.

Eventually, the whole outfit – Adkins, the dogs, the sleds, everything – had to be evacuated by air. They were flown to Nome where Adkins swore he was done with Iditarod.

The next year he was back, and he did 13 Iditarods thereafter, the last in 2006. He even ran Iditarod through a period when he was suffering from so much back pain he hobbled around like a grimacing humpback. He continues to run dogs to this day. A former winner of the John Beargrease Sled Dog Race in Minnesota, the now 62-year-old Adkins was planning to run the 2010 Iditarod, but pulled out at the last moment. His son, Chris, 41, did compete, however. Chris finished 50th, and at one point – when struggling through an Iditarod rough patch of his own – was heard to lament that he'd been tricked into it by his dad's idea that they do the Iditarod together because it would be fun. It can be, but it often isn't.

Barnum decided he'd had enough. He wasn't expecting to be back, but whether he will prove able to resist the pull is hard to say. There seems often to be that belief that "I could do better next time."

After Rogers broke his leg in his second Iditarod in 2007, he made that very observation. "So we refinanced our house to get the money for the 2008 race," he wrote. "I...finished 68 (again) out of 78 finishers and 96 starters (but) I'm finally getting the idea. Two weeks later, the dogs and I ran the Taiga 300, finishing with a 110-mile run to take second place and the vet's choice award for excellence in dog care. This is what life is all about, living your dreams and following your passion. I just need a way to pay for it."

The other alternative is, of course, to get out. Barnum left Iditarod 2010 at least planning to explore that option.

5

Finger Lake to Rainy Pass

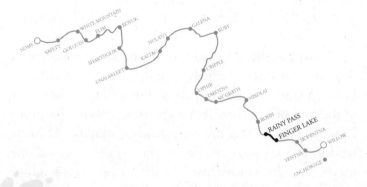

Less than 150 miles north of Willow, the Iditarod Trail beyond Winterlake Lodge at Finger Lake has long lived in infamy. Back in the 1980s and early 1990s when ABC television filmed the race for its popular "Wide World of Sports" program, Iditarod champ Rick Swenson sometimes accused cinematographers of waiting in the dark at Red Lake below the lodge to flash bright lights in the eyes of mushers and cause them to crash their sleds.

Not that any extra effort is really necessary to cause sleds to crash along this stretch of trail. Almost at the backdoor of the lodge begins a bobsled run down hill. Often the snow at aptly named Winterlake is piled six- to 10-feet deep and the so-called "wells" beneath the boughs of the spruce trees along the trail can suck in and crash a sled even before the bottom of the hill is reached.

If not, there's a sharp left-hand turn just before the lake that has been known to get more than a few mushers. It is especially gnarly for the back of the packers because most of the sleds in front of them have been driven by terrified mushers standing on what is called a drag brake. The drag brake is a piece of snowmachine track lashed between the runners of the sled. It is designed to eat into snowy trail and slow the team. It does the former very well, the latter marginally so.

Unfortunately, for those farther back in the Iditarod field, the snow-eating efficiency of the drags that have gone before will sometimes have chewed out a rut in the center of the trail two or three feet deep. This presents two problems. The first is that the rut is hard to straddle. Mushers tend to end up with one sled runner in the hole and one up on the side, which causes the sled to tip. Strong mushers can manhandle the sled through. The weak crash. The Iditarod Trail is never kind to the weak.

Then again, sometimes it's never kind to anyone. Even if a musher has the skill and luck to get a runner on either side of the rut, a second problem presents itself. The rut is sometimes so deep the drag brake won't reach the bottom, which means the only way to slow the sled is by dragging one's feet, which is both difficult and somewhat dangerous.

The dogs, of course, don't care. Given that they're going downhill and the going is easy, they will often jump their speed from a 10-mile-per-hour trot to a 15-mile-per-hour lope. It can be a wild ride just getting down that first hill, and all of this is only the beginning of the fun on the 35-mile run from Finger Lake to the next checkpoint at Rainy Pass.

Ahead there are the notorious steps down to the Happy

River, and then what is often nasty side-hilling along a bluff above the Happy going north. Iditarod veteran DeeDee Jonrowe from Willow, a two-time runnerup in the Iditarod, broke her hand along the latter section of trail when she crashed in 2007. Doug Swingley, a four-time champ, that same year cracked his ribs and dislocated a thumb. These were not unusual incidents.

Sue Morgan from Richmond, Utah, crashed out here in 2006 on her first try at Iditarod and nearly repeated that experience when she tried again in 2008. The second time through she scarred her face in a crash and bloodied her nose, but survived to eventually finish the race. North Dakota's Nancy Yoshida was not so lucky in her first Iditarod try in 2009. She broke both runners on her sled, and then in the confusion of a dog tangle while trying to get that fixed, she lost a dog named Nigel. He ran on up the trail. It took her days to catch him, and by then her Iditarod was over. Yoshida said later that friend Vern Halter, a transplanted Dakotan and veteran of 18 Iditarods, warned her about the trail to Rainy Pass. His warning, she added, came nowhere close to the indescribable reality.

Blame for much of this can probably be placed on Gene Leonard, the colorful squatter who showed up at Finger Lake in the early 1970s. He built a cabin along the lake and started eeking out a living as a trapper. His trapline dropped down to Red Lake and then took off into a complex of beaver dams and beaver ponds that ran nearly all the way to the Happy River steps. It was good country for trapping.

When the first Iditarod was being planned in 1973, Leonard helped the U.S. Army establish the race trail. Not surprisingly, he led them down the only established trail in the area – his trapline – instead of hunting for the old Iditarod route to the west. Over the years, Leonard's trapline trail to the Happy became the established route for the Iditarod race. Today, the true historic trail is little used, though it passes through more forgiving terrain to the Skwentna River to the west and then up along the river past the long-gone Mountain Climber Roadhouse to where the route rejoins the existing trail near the Happy River confluence. The historic trail avoided the now infamous Happy River steps, which have over the history of the Iditarod Trail Sled Dog Race provided the backdrop for so much film, video and photography of rolling and crashed dog sleds.

Most accounts of the Iditarod Trail of gold rush days portray a friendlier trail from Finger Lake to Rainy Pass than exists today, though the late Don Bowers, an Iditarod historian, wrote in his trail notes that "even the original Iditarod sometimes changed its routing from year to year. For instance, the trail up from the Skwentna River to Shirley Lake took at least two different routes, and one alternate route from the vicinity of Finger Lake went all the way to the Rainy Pass Lodge area on the north side of Happy River, bypassing the Steps, the (Shirley Lake) Hill, and even notorious Round Mountain."

Possibly in keeping with this tradition of changing routes, the modern trail still shifts a bit from year to year. Swing the beam of a headlight around in the dark down along the beaver ponds between Red Lake and the Happy, and it will often light up trail-marking reflectors from one side of the valley to the other. All were nailed to trees to mark the position of the ever shifting trail from winter to winter. Some of the reflectors are 10 or 15 feet high. Those were nailed up in deep-snow winters. Others are only three or four feet off the ground.

There have clearly been a lot of different trails in basically the same place through this patch of Alaska over the years, but all can be traced back to Leonard. He was one of those characters who enriched the trail and was enriched by it. He died only four years after abandoning his cabin at Finger to move back to Tennessee in 1990 with his wife, June. She was a mailorder bride who became Gene's long-suffering assistant through the many years their tiny home served as the Iditarod checkpoint. The place would regularly end up so crowded with mushers there was barely room to turn around, but June managed always to keep a smile on her face. In 2006, two years after Leonard's death, the four-time Iditarod race veteran was named the year's honorary dog driver. The pre-race proclamation noted he "knew all the trails in the (Finger Lake) area and was a valuable adviser to the mushers and race officials."

After the Leonards left for Tennessee, the Finger Lake checkpoint made do for years with nothing but tents. Brothers Bud and Dennis Branham, a pair of big game guides, then owned what was to become Winterlake Lodge, and they didn't like the Iditarod much more than they had liked the Leonards. The Iditarod's makeshift tent camp at Finger nearly caused the first fatality in Iditarod history. A propane heater being used to warm one of the tents in 1994 filled the structure with deadly carbon monoxide. Had not one musher sleeping there awakened and realized what was happening, any of the four others in the tent might have died.

As it was, two had to be revived and one, citing long term physical damage from the incident, eventually sued the Iditarod for the cost of her care. There are still tents in use at Finger Lake, but they are now heated by stoves vented to the outside, and the checkpoint in general has become a lot more comfortable since the Dixons, Kirsten and Carl, bought the lodge, expanded it and embraced the race. Kirsten is a world-class chef, who oversees a world-class kitchen staff with assistance from daughter Mandy. A musher who walks into this kitchen is likely to be handed the best-tasting bowl of soup he or she will ever wrap hands around.

It's almost enough to make an Iditarod veteran want to stay and spend the winter, given the way the trail ahead looms ominous. Most years, mushers know almost anyone's race can end out there in one unexpected crash. So intimidating is the trail to Rainy that it alters the race strategy of the Iditarod's top contenders. Mitch Seavey from Sterling, the 2004 Iditarod champ, said he would like to be able to start his team north at an easy pace and then pick it up steadily along the way, but he doesn't dare.

Hitting the Finger Lake-to-Rainy Pass section of trail too far back in the pack is too dangerous. The trail is too likely to be ripped up. There is too great a danger of crashing out in one of the holes left by the drag-braking riding mushers ahead.

It is an odd year when the trail to Rainy is in good shape. Thanks to Iditarod volunteer Roger Ashcroft, his sons and others, 2010 was one such odd year. The trail was as good – no, better – than any veteran musher ever remembered seeing it, and still it smashed the dreams of some.

6

Karin Hendrickson

Transplanted Californian Karin Hendrickson was one of the 2010 Iditarod mushers destined to fall victim to the Iditarod Trail on the climb into the Alaska Range. Three days into the race, the 39-year-old environmental regulator from the Anchorage suburb of Chugiak was supposed to be behind a dog team heading down the north side of the mountains toward a snug cabin near the confluence of the South Fork Kuskokwim and Tatina rivers. Instead, she found herself sitting at a long, pine table in the Rainy Pass lodge beside Puntilla Lake fighting to hold back tears as she talked about the death of her Iditarod dream.

An adventure-searching graduate of the University of Colorado at Boulder, Hendrickson had come to the Iditarod somewhat reluctantly. Her mother, Gwen Rodman, first urged her north. An Iditarod volunteer, Rodman lobbied Hendrickson to join her at work along the trail in 2002. Hendrickson gave in and came. She discovered she really enjoyed being around the dogs, and returned as a volunteer again in 2003. When she went back to America that year, she realized she didn't want to be back.

"....I knew my future," she wrote in her race biography.

"I sold my house and everything in it, quit my job and headed north." For two years, she apprenticed as a dog handler. Dog handlers are the serfs of the mushing world. They shovel dog crap, feed and water dogs, repair ripped harnesses and broken gear and eventually, if they are judged worthy, graduate to actually running dog teams.

Hendrickson was smart enough to see that this was, generally, a road to nowhere; so she got out, went to work making real money, and started building her own kennel. By 2009, she was in position to run her first Iditarod and finished a solid 40th.

She devoted the next year to training for her second Iditarod. That meant she had no life other than work and dogs. Even with help from husband Varay Hoyt, there was no time for more. For almost a year, Hendrickson and Hoyt poured money into dogs while Hendrickson trained and trained and trained some more. She spent so much time and effort training she actually began to think of Iditarod 2010 as a vacation.

"I work full time year-round," she said. "I work. I run dogs. I work. I run dogs. It's all for this. Mushers talk about being constantly broke, constantly tired. It's hard. The race is relaxation."

The 2010 Iditarod was supposed to be fun, and then there she was in Rainy Pass with the race leaving her behind and all of the fun draining out of the vision.

Outside the big picture windows in the lodge overlooking the lake, the winds blew snow sideways in the five-degree cold, and dog teams still in the Iditarod race started the long push toward the 3,350-foot pass that breaks through the Alaska Range. Hendrickson had the dog team to chase after them, but she didn't have the sled. It was in bits and pieces back along the trail to Finger.

Had she been just a little bit lucky, the weather would have been such that an airplane could fly a new sled to the checkpoint. But bad weather was keeping the planes grounded, and Hendrickson didn't learn until too late that the sled of fellow competitor Zoya DeNure was going to become available. DeNure was getting ready to drop out of the Iditarod because of a problem that could only be described as unprecedented.

"I've got an infection in my left breast," said the one-time international runway model. "Note to new moms in Iditarod: Wean your babies first. This is the dumbest thing I've ever done. My sled's in good shape. My dogs are in good shape. My head is good. I'm just in a lot of pain. I thought I could go," but doctors told her that idea was just plain stupid. DeNure didn't really want to heed their advice to go back to an Anchorage hospital and seek medical treatment, but she did.

"I did all my crying all ready," she said. "Now I can laugh."

When she knew she was going to have to quit, she offered her sled to Hendrickson, but by then it was too late. Hendrickson had already spent 20 hours in the checkpoint, and it didn't make any sense at that point to leave until taking her 24 mandatory rest. Race rules require all mushers make one, 24-hour stop somewhere along the 1,000-mile trail, and Hendrickson, recognizing her predicament with the sled, had shown the clarity of mind to declare hers at Rainy Pass. The problem was the 2010 race was screaming toward Nome at unprecedented speed.

"I'd be seven hours behind the last person going out of here," Hendrickson said, "and (Iditarod race officials are) not going to go for that." With the winds blowing snow sideways in Rainy Pass, race judge John "Andy" Anderson was telling mushers he wanted them to bunch up and work together to get through the notorious and narrow gap in the mountains. Hendrickson was pretty sure he'd fight her going over on her own, though she had faith it would be no problem for her dogs.

They were young and crazy two-year-olds in 2009. Now, they were strong and veteran three-year-olds. The problem wasn't with the dogs. The problem was with the musher.

"I don't want to be the last musher," Hendrickson said, again fighting back tears. "I feel like it's a cop out, but I don't want to keep going. Maybe next year. Next year, if I'm gonna do it again, I need money. I need sponsors."

Sponsors don't exactly line up to support mushers who finish worse in their second Iditarod than in their first. It's simply better business to back someone who looks like they might be on the way to becoming a winner instead of sliding backward like a loser. Thus there were good, practical reasons to quit, although that didn't exactly make the quitting any easier. DeNure, a pretty and soft-spoken woman, tried to counsel her friend Hendrickson.

"You can travel around home (with the dogs) if you just want to travel," she said. Hendrickson nodded and ran her fingers through her long, dark hair. She struggled to keep her heartbreak from being too obvious.

If only she'd made it to Rainy with a sled instead of half a sled, she said. If only she'd thought about what would happen if she broke the tail off her tail-dragger on that notorious stretch of trail between Finger and Rainy. If only the curse of bad luck had gone elsewhere. She still couldn't quite believe her sled had broken.

"I'm going across this flat area," she said, "and then I hear this crunch, crunch."

That was the sound of both of sled runners snapping beneath her feet. That was the precursor to her being forced to finally rip the entire rear compartment off her tail-dragger sled. Absent the tail that provided a seat and stored gear, the sled looked a lot like an old-fashioned Iditarod toboggan, but it only held half as much gear. No matter how things looked, the front half of a sled was still only half a sled.

"The problem is I never thought about that," Hendrickson said. "I couldn't get all the gear in the front." She squeezed in what she could, lashed some more to the outside, tossed the rest, and pushed on. She made the Rainy checkpoint fine, but with only half a sled there was a big problem ahead.

"I could get to Rohn," Hendrickson said, "but I couldn't get across the Burn."

It is 75 miles across the former Farewell Burn from the outpost cabin of Rohn to the Interior village of Nikolai. Mushers need to be able to carry enough food to feed a team at least once along the way. Hendrickson's half-a-sled couldn't hold the dog food, and she wasn't about to starve her dogs on the run to Nikolai. The dogs were her children, her friends.

"God, they're so strong," she said. "They're so good this year. It was going so great."

There she had to stop and struggle again to hold back the tears. She pushed back her chair and got up from the table, unable to talk anymore.

"I gotta go do something to get my dogs out of the wind," she said, leaving to be alone with her best friends and her shattered dream. They were all heading south as the Iditarod continued north.

7

Michael Suprenant

Over the course of almost 40 years, the makeup of the field entered in the Iditarod Trail Sled Dog Race has changed steadily and greatly. In the beginning, the race attracted mainly those who lived and worked, often with dogs, in rural Alaska. First Iditarod champ Dick Wilmarth was a gold miner and trapper from Red Devil in the frozen Interior of the state who cobbled together some huskies from villages along the Kuskokwim River for the run. He didn't really expect to win the inaugural race, but he did. The people who followed Wilmarth along the trail for the next few years were a lot like him.

The top 10 finishers in 1980 were a retired merchant marine captain turned Bush rat from Trapper Creek, a power plant operator from McGrath, an ivory carver from Shishmaref, a gold miner from Manley, an understudy of race founder Joe Redington from Knik, a builder from Kotzebue, a former VISTA volunteer from St. Michael, a hippy from Talkeetna, a trapper and fisherman from Ruby, and a homesteader from Skwentna. By 1990, though, the race was changing; the top 10 that year comprised five professional mushers, or budding professionals; a printer from

Wasilla, a commercial fisherman from the Kenai Peninsula, a farm boy from Minnesota, a state fisheries biologist, and the last of the old-time, blue-collar Native mushers.

Still, the Iditarod itself was clearly transitioning from an esoteric event for an odd bunch of Alaska sled dog fanciers to a race for professionals and adventurers with money or access to deep-pocket sponsors. The trend only continued as race entry fees skyrocketed along with the costs to enter qualifying races that soon came to be required just to get into Iditarod. Thus the 2010 race was heavy with those in the business of raising or racing sled dogs or both, and those who could afford to pay $40,000 to $85,000 to lease a team.

Still, there were a few throwbacks like Mike Suprenant of Chugiak. One of those lunch-bucket guys who caught the Iditarod bug and couldn't shake it, Suprenant held pancake feeds to try to raise money for the adventure and posted online his monetary needs in case anyone wanted to help sponsor something like the entry fee, $4,600; or dog booties, $1,500; or vet fees, $1,000; or simply sled-runner plastic, $50 per set, but with a new set pretty much needed at each of about 20 checkpoints.

The top mushers usually send multiple sets of plastic to checkpoints, so they can pick the plastic that will slide best in given snow conditions: Dark grey for extreme cold; light grey for warm, sticky snow; or yellow for average conditions. Suprenant couldn't afford that luxury. He was hoping on just one set of plastic runners of any kind at each checkpoint. He was as short on money as he was on time, but he was running anyway.

A 45-year-old retired avionics technician for the U.S. Air Force, Suprenant didn't make nearly enough money off his retirement to support a dog team. So he held a 7 a.m. to 5 p.m. job with the U.S. Army Corp of Engineers at Fort Richardson. The job was at least close to home. It allowed him to rise at 5 a.m., get his dog chores done, go to work, and get home in time to take the dogs for a nightly run. He prided himself on how he trained his huskies to jump into their boxes on his truck to save time. He could, he said, get the dogs loaded, trucked to the nearby dog trails, unloaded and hooked to a sled in 40 to 50 minutes. That allowed the opportunity to spend the next two to five hours running anything from 20 to 50 miles. Then Suprenant would truck them all home, unload and get to bed around midnight.

Veteran Iditarod reporter Kevin Klott described Suprenant's operation as the classic "mom-and-pop, small-market franchise... He found his handler on Craigslist, and she works practically free just to give her house dog, Nanook, some canine friends."

The handler was mainly an assistant poop scooper and dog feeder. Suprenant appreciated everything she did, but recognized the handicap of doing without a real partner to help run his 20 dogs.

"It's crazy," he confessed. "The sled dog thing is pretty addictive. I get by on five hours sleep."

Twenty dogs are about all one musher with a job can hope to train, and yet 20 dogs are barely enough to field an Iditarod team of 16. Come race day, there aren't a lot of choices to be made as to who goes to Nome and who doesn't. Healthy dogs are in; any dogs with injuries or health problems are out. Hopefully there will be 16 healthy and free of nagging injuries – sore wrists, sore shoulders, that sort of thing.

Suprenant first tried to get a dog team to Nome in 2008.

He made it as far as Golovin on the Bering Sea, 100 miles shy of Nome, before his dogs decided they'd had enough, and he called it a race. He came back in 2009 and did better. His team was the 49th to reach Nome. He beat the red lantern, the prize given to the last one in Nome, by two positions that year.

Like every back of the pack Iditarod runner, he hoped to do better this time. It is the eternal dream, and Suprenant's 2010 run to Nome was going fine until within about five miles of the Rainy Pass checkpoint. Among the last few teams to make the run up from Finger, he paid the price for coming late. He found one of those drag-brake-dug ruts next to a stump once buried in the trail.

"The runners, of course, went into the hole," Suprenant said. His sled hung up on the stump by its brake bar. Suprenant responded quickly. Even as he yelled at the dogs to "whoa," he was grabbing his snow hook and sinking it into the trail. He got the team anchored while there was still just enough slack in the gangline that he could pull the sled back an inch or two, tilt it up onto one runner and pop it off the stump. For a fraction of a second after, everything looked fine, and then Suprenant's foot bumped the snowhook.

"The dogs felt it give," he said. They took that as a signal to do what sled dogs love to do: Run. They charged ahead. The jerk tipped the already tilted sled over on its side. Suprenant clung to the handlebar in firm adherence to the prime directive of all mushing: Never let get of the sled. Never ever.

"So I'm getting dragged because I'm still holding on," Suprenant said.

He didn't really see the tree coming. He sensed it more

than anything before his head hit it, and then there was no not-letting go of the sled. The impact peeled him off. Only later would he discover he'd hit with such force the zipper of his mushing suit was embedded in his neck. He still doesn't know how long it took after the collision to gather his senses, but he did eventually get up and start walking down the trail in pursuit of his dogs.

He remembers Zoya DeNure and her dogs caught up and gave him a ride for a while. He believes John Stewart, the Scotsman, chased down the newly overloaded DeNure team and took over the musher-hauling duties.

He knows a crew from the Iditarod checkpoint in Rainy Pass, having caught Suprenant's runaway team there, finally came out by snowmachine to find him and then took over the task of hauling him back to the checkpoint. A volunteer veterinarian, who also happened to be a doctor, examined Suprenant and told him he had a concussion. Like Karin Hendrickson, Suprenant thought about taking his 24-hour layover in Rainy Pass to recover from the accident before pressing on. But he eventually chose to abandon the race instead.

"The Iditarod asked me not to (go on)," he said. "I got up the next morning and I had a pretty good headache even though I'd taken a lot of Motrin. I was still pretty loopy for a day. It was not the way I wanted to go out."

Prior to Iditarod 2010, Suprenant was pretty sure it would be his last year. Afterward, despite the blow to the head or maybe because of it, he was talking about buying a few new dogs from Jeff King, who'd announced his Iditarod retirement, and sounding a lot like a musher planning to be back.

"I believe I'm going to have to have somebody who will

help me out," he said. "But if I save up a lot of my comp and credit time, and I've got my vacation time...."

And if, of course, he can get by on five hours sleep for another winter and have no life but dogs and not go broke, well, then maybe the dream that died in 2010 could be reborn in 2011. For an Iditarod musher, there is always tomorrow.

8

Rohn to McGrath

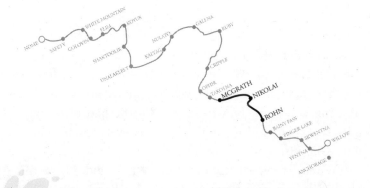

From the base of Lookout Mountain just beyond Puntilla Lake at the toe of the Alaska Range, the Iditarod Trail tracks north and west across Ptarmigan Valley into some of the most spectacular scenery in the 49th state. The big valley of the upper Happy River sprawls across low, rolling hills to meet mountains that claw for thousands of feet into the sky on either side. Ahead on the trail, a musher stares at another wall of mountains rising for more than a mile.

A rookie is likely to wonder about the route to the Rohn checkpoint 35 miles ahead because the 3,350-foot gap leading through the mountains and down to the notoriously problematic Dalzell Gorge is by no means obvious.

If, of course, anything is visible. Often it is not. The pass is fabled for its scenery-obscuring ground blizzards. Alaska musher Bobby Lee got caught in one in 1987 and thought he was going to die. Washington state musher Scott White nearly did so in 2007. He spent five hours out in the valley searching for the widely spaced tripods that mark the trail. On a clear day, the tripods are easy to see. In blowing snow or at night, or in a combination of both, they can disappear.

They disappeared in front of White in 2007. He and his team got lost. They wandered off the trail and floundered in deep snow. The dogs grew frustrated. "They were fighting and chewing," White recalled later. "Four got loose." Luckily, they came to White when he yelled at them in the howling wind and blowing snow, but he had to struggle to make repairs to his gangline and get everyone back into line. That just made things worse.

"When I took off my mittens," White said, "I frostbit my hands." A musher unable to use his hands because of frostbite is in serious danger. White recognized that. When his dogs finally found the trail, he did the sensible thing and turned them back toward the checkpoint. They all quit there. Everyone went home to Woodinville, Washington, to heal. White remembers well the weeks with sore, frostbitten hands that followed.

"I lost all the skin on my fingers at least five times," he said. Eventually, though, the fingers healed, and White returned to the 2010 Iditarod looking to redeem himself. His second attempt led him smack into another Rainy Pass maelstrom. When White arrived at the checkpoint on Puntilla Lake in the dark of night, the winds were steadily building. The blow sent dog booties and dishes rolling along the snow-covered ice. Other mushers were talking about waiting until dawn to try the pass ahead. White had

tried the waiting game three years earlier. There was no way
he was going to wait again. He headed out onto the trail.

"It was the exact same as 2007," he said. "I was like oh-
my-God I cannot believe it's the same. But there was one
key difference. I could see my dogs and I could see the trail
markers. Being able to see made a difference."

Between the few tripods that permanently mark the
Iditarod route, Iditarod trailbreakers had jammed into
the snow dozens of sticks of lathe topped with ribbon and
reflective tap. The reflective tape smiled back at White
in the beam of his headlamp as he worked his way trail
marker to trail marker into Ptarmigan Valley, across the
Happy River, up Pass Creek, over Rainy Pass, and down
Pass Fork Creek.

The trail there on the north side of the Alaska Range is
better than that on the south if for no other reason than
that it is easier to find. It drops through a canyon, crosses a
half-mile wide band of spruce forest just before the confluence of the Pass Fork and Dalzell creeks, slithers along the
creek ice, ducks back into the woods, climbs up a big hill
toward where the historic trail built by the Alaska Road
Commission cuts across a mountainside above the Dalzell
Gorge, and then dives into the gorge.

The descent is tricky. The trail down on the creek can be
just as bad or worse. The gorge is seldom more than 50 feet
wide. The creek winds between its rock walls. The creek
bed eats up 40 feet or more of the 50 feet of space. The
trail follows icy shorelines sometimes little more than a dog
sled wide. It is forced back and forth, back and forth on ice
bridges across the creek as it tries to link the usable pieces
of shoreline. Often there are gaping openings to flowing
water three to five feet down in the creek ice on either side

of the slippery icy bridges.

Mushers are advised to avoid thoughts about what could go wrong and just let the dogs run, because if they can only get through the Gorge everything gets easier. Once out on the ice of the Tatina River, it's smooth running to the Rohn checkpoint, and from there on all the way to McGrath the trail is sometimes likely to be rough, but no longer sled-smashing dangerous.

The latter is a relatively recent development. There was a time when the "buffalo tunnel" north of Rohn, the Post River "glacier," and the Farewell Burn all created big headaches for mushers. The sled-wide "buffalo tunnel," so named for the bison that roamed the area, between Rohn and pyramid-shaped Egypt Mountain were widened more than a decade ago. A trail was built to skirt the worst of the "glacier," which isn't really a glacier at all but a series of water-seeping muskegs that coat a hillside with ice. And the Burn is no longer a burn.

The 1.5-million-acre swatch of the Interior scorched by a wildfire in 1978 has now regrown. The trees still aren't big, but they're big enough to block the winds that swept the blackened wasteland of old. The scouring winds were what gave the one-time Burn a bad reputation for so long. Where they didn't blow the terrain bare, they created big, rock hard, sled-bashing drifts. The drifts were probably the worst of it. Particularly where they were on side hills, they made for difficult sled riding, and where they were deeply scarred by mushers standing on the drag brake, they could become almost impossible to navigate.

Mushers on the Iditarod saw none of this in 2010. Snow was thin on the trail out across the South Fork Kuskokwim ice into the buffalo tunnel, but there wasn't even the track of the bison that can confront a dog team there. Snow was even thinner from the Post River on to Egypt Mountain, but there was snow, which there often is not.

Between a U.S. Bureau of Land Management cabin a mile or so off the trail at Bear Creek and a bridge across the open water of Sullivan Creek, about 10 miles farther on, there was almost no snow and many frozen tussocks. It was rough and a problem for the dogs. There were an inordinate number of sprained ankles and shoulders along this stretch of trail, but there were no injured mushers and few broken sleds.

Beyond Sullivan Creek, meanwhile, the trail resembled an icy sidewalk that just kept getting better toward Nikolai and even better heading west for McGrath. Nikolai to McGrath, in fact, might have offered the smoothest trail of all for Iditarod 2010, but there were those who never got to enjoy it.

9

Pat Moon

By the time Iditarod rookies Pat Moon from Chicago and Kathleen Frederick from Willow left Puntilla Lake for Rainy Pass in the light of a new day, the ground blizzard that pummeled the Alaska Range the night before was winding down. The wind had stopped raging. The sky overhead was blue with clouds racing across it. But the trail was worse than it had been before. The wind had moved a lot of snow overnight.

What had been a dog-team-friendly trench three feet wide and two feet deep from near the crossing of the Happy River up along Fork Creek toward the 3,350-foot gap through the mountains was now a ditch only 12 to 18 inches wide and two feet deep. A sled wouldn't fit in that ditch. The sled kicked up on one side, tipped over, bounced out, and slammed into willows and trail markers.

The 130-pound Moon was in no shape for this. He'd never been a particularly strong guy to begin with. Since the age of 15, he'd battled with ulcerative colitis, an auto-immune disease that even when treated tends to leave people struggling with fatigue and weakness. Then came the February 2009 diagnosis that he had non-Hodgkin lymphoma, a nasty cancer. Almost half the people who contract that disease die within five years.

Moon started chemotherapy to treat it, but refused to let go of the Iditarod dream he'd been pursuing since taking an Idita-ride through the streets of Anchorage in a dog sled in 2006.

When it came time to choose between the Iditarod and treatment, he took a break from the latter to pursue the former. The 33-year-old Loyola University grad wanted, he said, to show children and others that they should never give up their dreams. His aim, proclaimed the Team Moon Dog Sled Racing website, was to "prove to anyone that has an illness or affliction that anything is possible."

Almost 100 years before Moon hit the trail, one of the grand, old men of Alaska sled dog travel, Archdeacon Hudson Stuck, had made his own observation of what is possible. "The old timers in Alaska have a saying," Stuck wrote in 1914 in the book *Ten Thousands Miles with a Dogsled,* "that traveling at 50 degrees below is all right as long as it is all right."

Those words can be applied to many things a man or woman contemplates or encounters in the mountains and wilds of Alaska. Everything is all right as long as it is all right. Anything is possible right up until the moment it becomes impossible. Moon did not know it, but he was heading toward the impossible as he finally topped Rainy Pass and came pin-balling down Pass Fork Creek, his sled hitting willows growing ever bigger as the trail dropped from the tundra into the brush headed for the spruce forest below.

Partially by the luck of an old avalanche that had wiped out a big stand of spruce along the trail, Moon made it almost to Dalzell Creek before his sled encountered a tree big enough to do serious damage. A musher healthier and stronger than Moon might have been able to tilt the sled as it rounded a gentle corner and slid toward that tree. Tipped toward the runner on the inside of the curve and weighted to the inside, the sled would have merely tapped the tree trunk, caromed off and continued safely on its way.

Moon, however, wasn't really in any condition to do that. He was more riding the sled than steering it. He was standing tall on the runners when the left one caught the tree. The impact and the sudden redirection of the sled slapped him head first into the spruce. He was knocked cold.

Not long thereafter, Belgian musher Sam Deltour, a medical student, found Moon on his back in the middle of the trail. Deltour thought for a minute that Moon might be dead, and then reacted like the musher the family of former race champ Mitch Seavey had trained him to be. He went past Moon's body to secure the dog team so no dogs would get hurt. Moon was sliding back into reality as Deltour finished that task.

"I woke up," Moon said later. "Sam was sitting there tying off. I said, 'Hey Sam.'"

Deltour was as happy to hear those words as much as Moon was happy to say them. The Belgian helped Moon move his team to an open area near the confluence of the Pass Fork and Dalzell Creek and park it. Then Deltour took off as fast as his dogs could go down through the Dalzell Gorge for Rohn to get help.

As he was heading south toward Rohn, Steve Perrin Jr. and a cameraman filming a reality show about the Perrin family's Rainy Pass Lodge were heading back south on snowmachines. They found Moon and took over his care until a small, single-engine plane on skis dropped out of the sky and landed on a snow-covered gravel bar near the confluence of the creeks.

By then a still shaken Moon had decided he'd had enough of the Iditarod. "I'm gonna call it a career," he said, standing in the middle of the trail with his face bruised and streaked with blood. Even before taking the opportunity to consult with Iditarod race judge Kevin Saiki and a race veterinarian, the closest thing to a medical professional in the area at the time, Moon was ready to go home. He waited for them to walk over from the airplane.

Moon told Saiki he was ready read to quit. Saiki didn't try to talk him out of it. Though Moon's pupils were acting normally and he seemed coherent, everyone was concerned by the fact he couldn't remember the crash or much of what followed. Saiki figured the best idea was to get the musher to a clinic as fast as possible. Moon concurred.

"I just woke up," he said, "and there I was. I don't think I'm in a position to make a decision on what to do."

Everyone nodded in agreement. An Iditarod veteran, Saiki offered to steer Moon's dog team down to Rohn if the musher got on the airplane. Moon thought that was great. The dogs were resting quietly in the snow along the creek. Moon was alert enough to remember who was in lead at the front of the team he'd leased from Michigan's Ed Stielstra and spent seven months training.

"Luke and Lou," he told Saiki, "they'll take you anywhere you want to go."

"I apologize to the Iditarod," he added.

"That's OK," Saiki said.

Moon repeated the apology a few more times. Some

people, he said, thought he shouldn't be on the trail in his condition. He hadn't wanted to be a problem, he said, but he thought it important to try to chase his dream.

"Don't apologize," Saiki said. "Let's just get you into McGrath and have you looked at."

The small clinic at McGrath to the north of the Alaska Range seemed at the time the best option. Weather to the south had been limiting flights to Anchorage, but by the time Moon was in the air the skies to the south were clearing. A pilot with the all-volunteer Iditarod Air Force sped him toward an Anchorage hospital even as Saiki was delivering the dogs toward Rohn.

Moon would eventually recover. Saiki, meanwhile, would get back to Rohn in plenty of time to begin a long and baffling wait for Frederick, the musher at the tail-end of a snaking string of Iditarod teams that at that moment stretched for more than 200 miles from race leader John Baker on the trail out of Ophir in the Interior, back over the mountain to Takotna, up the Kuskokwim River to McGrath, east to Nikolai, and then south again across the Farewell Hills, the Farewell lakes and the snowless Post River country to the lonely Rohn checkpoint sandwiched between the Terra Cotta and Teocalli mountains deep in the Alaska Range.

10

Kathleen Frederick

Long before Kathleen Frederick started the descent from Rainy Pass down along the sometimes avalanche-threatened Pass Fork Creek toward the Dalzell Gorge, a narrow and notorious gap that snakes through the Teocalli Mountains, this infamous stretch of trail had nearly claimed its first victim in Iditarod 2010. Thirty-seven-old Celeste Davis, a nurse from Deer Lodge, Montana, safely made it across the first, tricky ice bridges over open water, up and down sled-buster hill, and back across some more tricky ice bridges before disaster caught her just short of the safety of the wide, flat Tatina River. All it took for her run to go from perfectly fine to nightmarishly bad was the blink of an eye.

A sled runner caught on something in the ice beneath a thin skim of snow covering the trail. The sled went over. And suddenly Davis found herself being towed on her face through the Dalzell Gorge by a runaway dog team. The daughter of longtime Montana musher Bill Smith, she had since childhood been indoctrinated in the first rule of mushing: Never let go of the sled! Never let go of the sled! Never let go of the sled!

A stump in the trail disabused her of that idea. The stump

caught her square between the eyes at a speed approaching 15 miles per hour. Her nose shattered. Whether she lost consciousness she doesn't know. She did finally let go. When she struggled to her knees, there was blood everywhere.

It was spraying out her nose. It was running down her throat. She thought at first she might choke on it. When she finally quit coughing and spitting out blood, and realized she could keep her airway clear to breathe, she wondered if she might still bleed to death. She knew she had to stop the bleeding somehow. She grabbed for the end of her nose and tried to pinch off the flow. That didn't work. So she grabbed at it between her eyes and pinched there. She felt bone move, but hung on. The bleeding began to ease and finally stopped.

Davis was lucky to find her team just ahead, anchored in place by her sled caught in some trees. She was lucky to get some help from another musher in freeing the sled and getting back on the runners. She was lucky that she was nearly out of the Dalzell and all that was left of the trail was five flat, easy miles down the smooth Tatina ice to Rohn where she lurked around the Rohn checkpoint for nine hours in pain and looking God-awful. The center of her face had by then swollen to twice its normal size and turned bluish black. Between that and her blonde-brown hair in corn rows and the way she sort of shuffled around head down and hunch-backed never saying anything, she could well have been auditioning for the part of a background character in a bar in a Star Wars movie. She would confess later she was moving so strangely because she was worried any sudden movement would shake loose the clot in her nose, and she'd start bleeding all over again. Her timid quietness, meanwhile, was obviously due to her being seriously concussed. In her normal state, Davis tends toward talkative and laughing.

One can fairly wonder if Davis should even have been allowed to continue along the trail in her condition, but the Iditarod doesn't worry much about such things. It is a dog race. The focus is on the dogs. They get looked over by small armies of veterinarians in every checkpoint. Not so the people. Nobody even suggested to Davis she seek medical attention. Checkers mainly tried to hurry her on along the trial. She was packing to leave when Frederick finally made her long-awaited appearance.

For hours, Iditarod volunteers at Rohn had wondered what was happening with Frederick on the 35-mile trail over the mountains from Puntilla Lake. Weather did not seem to be a problem, but what had been for most mushers a four- to five-hour run from the previous checkpoint was stretching to seven, eight and finally more than nine hours for Frederick. Several times the Rohn checkpoint, which had only a satellite telephone for communications, messaged Iditarod headquarters in Anchorage asking for information from a GPS tracking device on Frederick's sled. The information that came back was confusing. At one point, everyone believed Frederick was five miles out of Rohn and doing three miles per hour. As it turned out, she was more like 5.3 miles out and stuck.

The 58-year-old dog driver had put her sled in the ditch or, more accurately, the creek. Dalzell Creek with its rotten ice and gaping holes had been waiting all race to snag somebody. One little mistake as Frederick rounded a corner in the Gorge and her Iditarod Trail Sled Dog Race was over.

Luckily, she had the sense to violate the mushing rule to which Davis had so tenaciously clung. Frederick let go of the sled at the edge of an abyss. It turned out to be a wise move given the sled was sliding sideways off an ice bridge toward a big hole. Frederick's dogs just made it across the ice. Her sled didn't. Sans musher, it went crashing into a five-foot deep slot in the ice and then wedged, upside down, in the water flowing beneath.

"It was ironic," Frederick said. "All my survival gear was in the sled, and I couldn't move it. It took five people to get it out."

The five people were Iditarod trail sweeps who follow along behind the end of the race every year to help out if necessary in cases just like this. Had they not arrived within hours of Frederick's accident, she could have been there all night, rolling over in her mind again and again what she might have done differently to avoid wrecking her Iditarod run.

The ice bridge that got her was a trap. Narrow and with big holes on either side, it came up quickly after a sharp left-hand corner. All that kept it from snagging any number of teams was the snow that fell just before the start of Iditarod 2010. That snow bonded to the glare-ice that served as the approach to the bridge. Sled drivers were able to brake just enough to make the corner. A race worth of traffic over the trail had, however, broken the bond between snow and ice by the time Frederick arrived.

"Actually, it was deceptive," she said, "because it looked like good snow. Normally, you see something like that and you slow down and it's fine."

Frederick tried to slow down. She stepped on the drag brake, that piece of snowmachine track mounted between the runners of her dog sled. One of two brakes on an Iditarod toboggan, the drag brake is designed for stopping in snow. It works pretty well for that.

Unfortunately, it doesn't work at all on ice. What Frederick should have stepped on was the ice brake, which drives a couple of spikes down into the ice to slow the sled. She realized this almost as soon as she stepped on the drag brake, and it started skidding over ice. She and the sled were suddenly being whip-cracked behind a team going fast around a corner onto an ice bridge. The sled started sliding sideways. The hole in the ice was coming fast. There was only one sensible thing to do: Jump!

Immediately after, things looked fine, at least for a moment. The dogs were all okay. The sled was down in a hole but basically intact.

"It would have been fine if the sled just hadn't flipped," Frederick said. Only it had flipped, and then it had wedged upside down under the shelf ice, and everything a five-foot, three-inch woman needed to get at to free the heavy sled – some rope, her ax, a couple carabineers to use as pulleys – was stuck in a sledbag Frederick couldn't reach.

"When I fell in the hole, I knew it was going to start a bad chain of events," she said. Eventually, she would need the help of those trail sweeps to get the sled out. Technically, she probably could have been disqualified after that for violating a race rule that bans so-called "outside assistance." But there really wasn't any other way to extract the sled, and she didn't want to leave her dog team camped out in the middle of the trail on the gangline for days trying.

When the sweeps offered to help her yank the sled out from under the ice, she accepted the help. And when race manager Mark Nordman later called her on the satellite phone at Rohn to suggest she drop out of the race, she scratched, and then cried and cried some more.

"I'm totally bummed out," she said. "I'm telling myself, 'I didn't get hurt. The dogs didn't get hurt.' But I'm totally bummed out."

Crying seemed to help, and a little rationalizing didn't hurt. "Not many women my age do something like this," she said. Not many men, either. And certainly not many who spent most of their lives in southeastern Pennsylvania.

Frederick – a former librarian, former teacher and now practicing attorney – didn't get to Alaska until she was 50, and even then she ended up in rainy, coastal Juneau, which might be the capital of the 49th state but is most definitely not the sled dog capital.

Never mind that, though, she was in Alaska at last, and since she was there she figured it was time to start the pursuit of the sled dog dream she'd had since going for a ride behind a team in Maine in 1996. A decade later, with help from nearby Canadian mushers and a handful in Southeast Alaska, Frederick started to work building a team for the Iditarod.

She had the scheme going along pretty well, too. She got her Iditarod qualifiers out of the way in 2009. She got good training on her dogs in 2010 and started her rookie Iditarod slow and easy with a plan to slowly move up.

"It was going great," she said. "I was cruising by the time I was going into Rohn. I was only going to stay here four or five hours."

She would have left still among the back of the pack, but her schedule would have put her well ahead of the red lantern, the award for finishing last. Instead, she never left at all. After getting her wet sled out of water flowing under the ice of Dalzell Creek, she pulled into the checkpoint late in the night with an ice-encased sled and ice-encased gear that must have been carrying 500 pounds of water, and a dog team unhappy about dragging this new, hefty load those last miles to Rohn.

"What a mess," Frederick said. "Everything's frozen. It's the first time; it's the last time. I can't afford this. I had to take off work. It exceeded my cost estimate. Next year, I only want to do the (Yukon) Quest 300-miler and the Percy de Wolf," a race from Dawson, Yukon Territory, Canada to Eagle, Alaska, and back.

"Now, I have to find a job and get back to work. This was a one-shot deal. That's what makes it so hard. I can't believe people do this year after year. It's so expensive."

More expensive than a drug habit, she noted, and possibly almost as addictive for some. Frederick could only hope that she was cured.

11

McGrath

Three-hundred-fifty miles north along the Iditarod Trail from the old port of Knik on Cook Inlet, the community of McGrath survives as an important demarcation point on the winding, 724-mile-long Kuskokwim River. The village traces its roots back to the Athabascan Indians who came from up river and down to trade here hundreds of years ago. The first white man to stay, Abraham Appel, arrived in 1904 to establish a trading post across the river from where the city now sits.

With the discovery of gold in the Innoko Mining District to the north, Old McGrath boomed. Situated near the end of navigation for the larger riverboats of the day, it was a convenient place to build a regional supply center. By 1907, the ragtag collection of buildings that sprouted up around the riverboat landing had taken the name of U.S. Marshal Peter McGrath. Travel along the Iditarod Trail would keep that McGrath thriving for a couple decades before the gold began to run out and the river shifted.

The winding of the Kuskokwim, even more than the decline of Alaska gold mining, put an end to Old McGrath. After a major flood in 1933, the town pretty much packed up and moved across the river to the south bank. The old riverboat landing on the north bank became useless. The Alaska Commercial Company built a new store on the south bank and what was left of the city regrouped around it and began looking for a new reason to exist. New McGrath grew as airplanes took over for sled dogs in Alaska. The Federal Aviation Administration arrived in 1940 to clear an airstrip and build a communications complex for advising pilots in the Interior. The growth in population led to the opening of a school.

Then came World War II, which changed things in a big way. The U.S. Lend-Lease Program was engaged in a major effort to ferry aircraft of all sorts from the Lower 48 states to the embattled Union of Soviet Socialist Republics. McGrath became an important refueling stop on the flight route. The airport got a mile-long runway. More than 400 soldiers moved in to swell the local population of about 200. By the end of the war, the community was established as a modern regional hub. The soldiers went home, but the civilian population steadily grew from a couple hundred people in 1950 to nearly 500 as gold soared toward $1,000 an ounce in the late 1970s and mining exploded all across Alaska once again. The population, however, peaked at 528 in 1990 and has been sliding ever since. It was reported at 317 people in 2008, and yet the community remains a pocket of civilization along the Iditarod Trail.

It has the expected amenities of a small town – hotels, bars, a restaurant, a cafe, a gas station, a grocery story, and a still busy airport. If you're a musher in the Iditarod Trail Sled Dog Race, this is a key place to contemplate whether to press on or give up. The toughest part of the trail is behind. Rookie mushers can find solace in that. They've survived the Happy River steps, the Dalzell Gorge, the Post River "glacier," and the Farewell Burn. None of which really presented much in the way of obstacles in 2010.

The steps were groomed so well it was all but impossible to roll a sled there. The Dalzell, which had been a nightmare of slick ice a week before the race, had gotten a coating of fresh snow that allowed everyone but late arrivals Celeste Davis and Kathleen Frederick to safely cruise through the s-curves winding back and forth over ice bridges above the creek. The so-called Post River "glacier," which isn't really a glacier at all but some overflow-prone muskegs that end up covered with a sloping sheet of ice, had enough snow sticking to it that the dogs could get traction to pull the sleds across. And the Burn – which was once an open wasteland where the wind either blew the snow away or piled it up into rock hard, sled-smashing drifts – was a second-growth forest bisected by a trail covered with just enough snow.

Granted, there was a 10-mile stretch of rough, snowless tussocks between Bear and Sullivan creeks that made for a sled-banging ride, but from there on it was pretty smooth running to the friendly, old, Athabascan village of Nikolai and on for another 55 miles to McGrath. The pile of broken dog sleds known to accumulate at the McGrath checkpoint in some years prior was non-existent. But there were broken mushers in McGrath – Iditarod veterans who knew that the though the toughest trail was behind them, the longest was still ahead.

From the banks of the Kuskokwim, or simply the "Kusko" as it is known to most in the Alaska Interior, the Iditarod Trail stretches out ahead for almost 350 long, somewhat boring, bitterly cold miles to Kaltag on the Yukon River. If a musher has a strong, fast team, this is the place to put some time into the field. Once over the 800-foot divide between the tiny village of Takotna and ghost town of Ophir, there are only rolling hills before the picturesque Yukon River village of Ruby, and from there the race course follows the smooth, frozen, snow-covered surface of Alaska's largest river for almost 150 miles west.

If you are back in the race pack, this is the place to begin to close the gap on those at the front. If, of course, you have the team to do it. If you don't have the team, or even think you don't have the team, you can only expect for the opposite to happen. The race in front will just keep getting farther and father away.

12

Linwood Fielder
and Karen Ramstead

Both Lindwood Fiedler from Willow and Karen Ramstead from Perryvale, Alberta, Canada, sat in the McGrath community center for a long time contemplating their sled dog futures. They were a pair of established Iditarod veterans, representing opposite ends of the Iditarod continuum. A breeder of Siberian husky show dogs, Ramstead was running her ninth Iditarod with no hope of winning, but then she'd never been in the race to win. She wanted only to show that the hairy, hefty, powerful huskies of yesteryear could still compete against the lean, short-coated, houndish sled dogs that have come to dominate the modern Iditarod. The descendants of the fictional lead dog of the fictional Sgt. Preston of the Royal Canadian Mounted Police – "On King! Mush you huskies!" – are, however, never going to beat what retired Iditarod champ Joe Runyan likes to call the "swifts."

The swifts rule the modern Iditarod, and Fiedler thought he had a championship-caliber team of them. A one-time social worker turned businessman, Fiedler was a sometimes Iditarod contender. Over the course of 17 Iditarods dating back to 1989, he had 11 times cracked the top 20. He first entered the top 10 in 1998, and in 2001 he led the race to the Yukon River and beyond. It looked for a time like he might win the that race, but he finished second to Montana's Doug Swingley, a four-time champ. Swingley retired in 2008 at the age of 54. After years of being brutalized by the trail and the weather, he'd had enough. Fiedler stayed in, despite being Swingley's age. Fiedler wanted just one of those Iditarod championships Swingley had in duplicates.

It was the ultimate dream for a man whose life had long before gone to the dogs, and it looked at times to be a dream tantalizingly close to within reach.

If Lance Mackey could win, how hard could it be? Mackey was as laid back as anyone you can find in sports today. Some might go so far as to say he sometimes appears a wee bit disorganized, even goofy. If Mackey can win the Iditarod, it should be easy for a well-organized, masters-degree-holding, sled dog businessman like Fiedler.

He's a professional manager. His sled dog camp on the Juneau Icefield above the state's capital city employs 20 people along with hundreds of dogs, and operates under environmental constraints fit for a nuclear power plant. He not only coordinates the maintenance of a dog kennel in an otherworldly environment and organizes daily flights for tourists wishing to ride a dog sled; he also oversees the world's largest dog-crap collection program. It daily cleans the glacier trails of droppings, loads them into 55-gallon drums and flies them away for disposal.

On top of this, there are the standard logistics of running a wilderness business – housing, supply and, maybe most of all, staffing. It is, in its way, a little like managing a dog team. You want to keep everyone well fed and working together, and Fiedler has proven a master of the art. He's a hugely successful businessman who entered the 2010 Iditarod confident he had the skills to win the dog race, and only one thing going against him – age. Jeff King is the only musher over 50 ever to win the Iditarod. Still Fiedler thought he had a shot.

His team was fast. He was out there running with the big dogs as the race rolled toward the Alaska Range. He led early, and then the wheels started falling off his carefully built racing machine.

"I started with a Ferrari," an embattled looking Fiedler said in McGrath, "and I went to a Ford."

Fast, carefully chosen dogs picked in part because they had been so injury free during training, started suffering injuries – a strained shoulder here, a sore wrist there. Pretty soon, instead of racing dogs up the trail, Fiedler was nursing dogs up the trail.

"The one thing I can't control is where the dogs put their feet," he said, and the dogs seemed to keep putting their feet in all the wrong places. Coming through the frozen tussocks that sprouted everywhere on the 10-mile stretch of trail between Bear and Sullivan creeks, Fiedler remembered watching dogs put their feet in holes and thinking, "No, no! Don't put your foot there!"

By the time Fiedler reached McGrath, he'd already dropped five injured dogs from the 16-dog team with which he started. He had a whole bunch more that needed to be dropped. Two of them were team leaders he was counting on to get him to Nome. They were well enough to trot with the team to the McGrath checkpoint, but not well enough to help pull. And there were two more like that.

"I'm really down to just seven cylinders," Fiedler said.

His Ferrari cum Ford was, he said, "now a Volkswagen with 80,000 miles."

There was clearly no way this outfit was going to catch the race leaders but Fiedler could have made it to Nome. Back in the day, he took an eight-dog team from Ophir, only 45 miles on up the trail, to the finish line.

"I ran every hill," he said, his weathered face breaking into a smile. ""I had a lot less gray hair then."

Despite the gray hair now, he was still capable of running every hill. He remained fit enough to out run most other members of the AARP in a foot race. The problem was that he didn't want to. He'd wanted to win the Iditarod, and that dream was gone for the year, gone quite possibly forever. He sat in McGrath trying to get his head around the idea that the time had come to quit, that the Iditarod had passed him by forever. There were a lot of younger men on the trail now behind strong teams.

"It's a tide of them," Fiedler said, "and they are very, very good."

The tide had swept over Fiedler. It was the same tide that had gone out and left Ramstead high and dry in McGrath contemplating whether she owned the Iditarod or the Iditarod owned her. Always before she had embraced her sled dog addiction, but this time it had taken her to rock bottom. She just wasn't having any fun anymore. She was struggling with a hand infected by the black spruce tree that speared through it; the trail was rough, as it usually is; her dogs seemed unhappy; and, her husband had been in a serious truck crash in Anchorage shortly after she left the city.

All of a sudden she found herself wondering why she was putting everyone in her life through the struggle.

"The Iditarod," she said, "is a pretty selfish endeavor."

By and large, mushers in the race give their all to the dogs. There often isn't much left for family or friends. Plenty try to get around this by dragging loved ones into the vortex. Ramstead trains with her husband, Mark, but the real love of the sport is hers, not his. The dogs have taken over her life and by extension theirs.

"My dogs are first and foremost our family," Karen said, "our pets." She has 65 to 70 pets. This, she admitted, is too many. She'd like to get down to 50 or so, which would permit some racing and allow her to continue to raise Siberian huskies for show.

While the vast majority of Iditarod mushers run so-called Alaska huskies – which trace their bloodlines back not only to Siberians but to a variety of bird dogs and hounds – the Ramsteads have stayed true to the old breed. Karen wraps herself in their history and their classic good looks. Over the years, she's had any number of prize-winning show dogs in her Iditarod teams. She is more than a little proud of the fact these beauty-pageant winners can still perform as the workhorses of the Arctic they were originally bred to be.

"There's good Siberian teams out there," she said. "I haven't finished last in a race since 2001."

As she talked about this at the McGrath checkpoint, Blake Freking from Finland, Minnesota, was far ahead on the trail with another team of purebred Siberians. She expected him to set a record for the breed once run by Martin Buser back in the 1980s. Then a young visitor to Alaska from Switzerland, Buser ran Siberians for Earl Norris from Willow, a legend in Alaska sled dog racing. Norris twice won the Anchorage Fur Rendezvous World Championship Sled Dog Race. Norris, like Ramstead, loved Siberians.

He stayed true to them long after fellow Fur Rendezvous champs Gareth Wright of Fairbanks and George Attla of Huslia started the move away in favor of breeds with smaller bones, longer legs and bigger lungs. Wright's "Aurora huskies" were a cross between Siberians and Irish setters with some hound and who-knows-what-else rolled in.

The Aurora huskies were long known to be great sprint-racing dogs, but there were questions about their ability to go the distance. Some questioned the toughness of their feet. Others said they would always be the hares bested in the end by the Iditarod-winning tortoises. Buser changed that thinking not long after he married Kathy Chapoton and split from the Norris's to build his own kennel near Big Lake. Some of the one-time "sprint dogs" were in Buser's team when he won his first Iditarod in 1992. They later helped him set the Iditarod record time of 8 days, 22 hours, 46 minutes in 2002. The record still stands.

The Siberians were fading from the scene well before Buser won, but he sealed the door on their history. Now, the only people who run them are those like Ramstead and Freking – mushers married to old, Jack Londonesque visions of the North – or those simply in love with the breed in the way people fall in love with all kinds of breeds from yappy Chihuahuas to lumbering Bernese mountain dogs.

Karen's only complaint about her Siberians was that they didn't live longer. The toughest part of being a dog musher, she said, is watching dogs, once sleek and powerful, age away to nothing.

"We have a substantial number of geriatrics in our kennel now," she said. "There are six over 13." They hang out in what she calls "geriatric park" where "they're on their own schedule."

Every year before leaving Alberta for Alaska to run Iditarod, Karen said, she takes some extra time in the park to play with and massage the old guys, and make sure they know how much she cares in case someone doesn't last until she makes it home.

Every year, she added, it gets harder to leave them behind. This year was especially bad.

"Usually I'm excited about going to Alaska in December to train," Karen said. "This time I didn't want to go. It's been hard to be gone from home this year."

And yet she couldn't stay away from Iditarod. Psychiatrists might say this is the definition of someone with a problem.

"I appreciate this is an addiction," Karen said.

Nine times she had run Iditarod. She started her first in 2000, but was forced to scratch. Since then she had finished four of seven. She owned four of the coveted Iditarod belt buckles awarded those who finish the race. It was hard to define her need to keep racing. She wasn't going to win. It would, in fact, take something of a miracle for her – or any other musher of Siberians, for that matter – to put a team in the Iditarod top 30.

Karen respected that. "Those top teams," she said, "they're moving it so far forward now in terms of what dogs can do."

Out at the front of the Iditarod, as she spoke, were 10 teams, give or take a couple, driven by mushers with the belief they had a shot at victory, and another 10 behind whose drivers were of the opinion they could show well in 2010 and, if all went according to plan, maybe win in 2011.

Back behind them were the teams with smaller expectations. Some wanted merely to accomplish one of the toughest challenges in sport. Others hoped to do more – finish in the top half, maybe. Certainly making it to Nome was the aspiration of all. Ramstead, in her fourth Iditarod, reached the finish line in 12 days, 8 hours. And in 2009, she bested that, reaching Nome in 12 days, 6 hours. She wouldn't quite admit to her goal for 2010, but it was pretty clear one of her expectations was to try to better 12 days. Freking, instead, was the one with the team on pace to do that and set a new record for purebred Siberians. He, not Ramstead, was destined to win a small place in Siberian husky history.

Early on, the older, heftier Siberian husky lover from Canada realized she wasn't going to hang with the younger, fitter man from Minnesota. She had too many things going against her, the infected hand, the training compromised by a sprained ankle, a dog team that hadn't been on enough camping trips.

"I wasn't happy with the way everything was going," she said as she sat at a long table in the crowded, noisy community center. "I was pleased with them, but after nine Iditarods, it's not enough just to move down the trail with them. I know what their limitations are (but) we were performing below my expectations. I think my team is capable with hanging with (Freking's).

"It's not the dogs' fault; it's my fault." Because of a sprained ankle slow to heal, Karen didn't spend much time out on extended camping trips with her dogs. Some of the younger animals inexperienced with camping on the trail were having trouble getting comfortable with that. The others just didn't seem to be having much fun. She decided to take the Iditarod's one required 24-hour stop in McGrath to see if things got better. There were a lot of calls to Mark during that time. She was constantly on the phone. She wanted to quit. Mark, she said, tried to talk her out of it.

But in the end, she gave it up.

"What's the definition of insanity?" she asked. "Doing the same thing over and over again and getting the same result? I don't think this will be my last Iditarod, but I do think the Iditarod is going to be scaled back in my life. My husband has picked up a lot for me."

He deserves a break, she said. She needed a break, she believed. Whether that happens remains to be seen. There are many on the Iditarod Trail now who have said in the past that they were done with the race, including Rick Swenson of Two Rivers, the race's only five-time champ.

Most who have tried to ease out of running the Iditarod have found it difficult. The only way to go seems to be to cut it off completely, to walk away and take the pledge never to come back. There are those – David Aisenbray, former contenders like John Cooper and Larry "Cowboy" Smith – who cured the addiction that way. Ramstead hoped for another solution. She quit the Iditarod wondering if she could become like that unique alcoholic who, having been cured, can go back to being a social drinker.

13

McGrath to Ruby

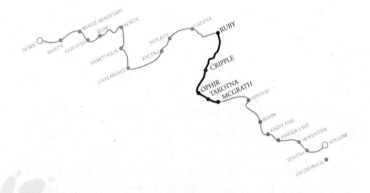

From McGrath on the Kuskokwim, the Iditarod Trail runs west for less than 20 miles through the forever-struggling community of Takotna before hooking north toward the heart of nothing. Once this land 400 miles north of Anchorage was promoted as the "Inland Empire." On Nov. 29, 1912, no less a source than the New York Times reported "thousands of miners from Fairbanks and all the lower Yukon and all the lower Yukon camps have been rushing into the Innoko creek for three months. Cripple City already rivals Fairbanks in population and in ambition to become the metropolis of Alaska."

It didn't happen. The gold petered out in decades. The miners started fleeing. The boomtown of Ophir just over the hill from Takotna went from 1,000 people shortly after the start of the 20th century to almost nobody 50 years later. The post office closed in 1957. By 1980, the official population was down to one. The community is now officially a ghost town.

All across the Empire, it was the same. The Poorman post office closed in 1952. Cripple City, also sometimes known as Cripple Landing on the Innoko, disappeared long before that. The same for the community of Long, Johnson's Roadhouse, 18 Mile Roadhouse, Lewis Roadhouse, California Roadhouse and the other one-time stops along the trail from the edge of the Kusko across the vast Interior to the Yukon at Ruby.

Millions of dollars in gold came out of the country, but when it was gone almost everything went with it save for some dredges and steam generators left to rust and some cabins, many of which were destined to burn down. Takotna somehow, though, managed to hang on. Once the port of supply for Ophir, it transitioned into a Cold War outpost in the 1950s and 1960s and then, as the Cold War was fading, went back to its wilderness roots to become the base of a Norwegian outdoor adventure camp.

Young Norwegians now fill the library that is the community center and restaurant, too, when the Iditarod rolls through in March. And the Newtons, Jan and husband, Dick, are still there. As they have been almost forever, or so it seems. The reality is that they are relative newcomers in the long history of the place. The Newtons arrived in the 1970s just before the Iditarod began. They had plans to run a lodge and explore the wilderness.

By the time they got there, Takotna was already well past its heyday. Established in 1908 as far up the Takotna River as Arthur Berry's small sternwheeler could go,

Berry Landing – later Portage City, Tocotna, Takotna City, Takotna Station and finally just plain old Takotna – boomed into the Roaring 20s. By the start of those years, Takotna was home to several mining-supply stores, a road-house, a post office, a newspaper and even, for a time in 1923, a radio station.

In 1921, the Alaska Road Commission built a good road over the mountain to Ophir and an airstrip. Another road to Sterling Landing on the Kusko was built in 1930 to make it easier to bring in supplies when the Takotna River was low, restricting riverboat access, but by then McGrath was already surpassing Takotna as the regional hub for the Kuskokwim Interior. Takotna hung on until construction started on the Tatalina Air Force Station seven miles to the south along the Sterling road. Tatlina grew as Cold War tensions heightened between the U.S. and the Soviets. For a time, a squadron of interceptor fighter jets was stationed at Tatalina, and a White Alice Communications System outpost on Takotna Mountain kept watch on Alaska skies with its radars. The Air Force even built a ski area for the troops on the slopes of the mountain, but by the 1980s the Air Force was pulling out and by 1994 it was gone.

Takotna remained as an outpost providing fuel and some supplies for the small number of miners who to this day come to work the Innoko country mines in the summer. There are still about 50 buildings clustered around Main Street in Takotna, too, but only half are occupied by the 50 or fewer residents. Still, it is home for a few like the Newtons who just can't bring themselves to leave, and a place to school a dozen children of the few parents still hanging on as trappers and miners in the area, and it is the base for that Norwegian folkehogskole.

Norwegian students who enroll in the Oyton Folk High School back home pay 56,000 Kroner (about $9,000) to go first to Alta in the north of Norway "to make the necessary preparations for the trip to Alaska," according to a school program. "We go to Alaska in the middle of February, where we start off with a week in Fairbanks. Here we will head out on our first skiing trips, visit a dog musher, and experience a little of the Alaskan life. Following the first week we will fly out into the Bush to the small, cut-off, Native American village of Takotna. This will be our base for the next four weeks. Together with local hunters and trappers, we will attempt the lives of the fur hunters, hunting and trapping various animals. The hunting and skiing conditions in the area are splendid. We will stay both in the village and in a hunters cabin out in the wilderness. In March, when the world's longest dog sled race, the Iditarod, starts, the village truly comes to life, being one of the checkpoints. During the race we'll take in the atmosphere and volunteer at the checkpoint."

By the time the Iditarod race arrived at Takotna in 2010, the place had swelled to twice its normal size with Norwegians, Iditarod officials and race veterinarians. The young Europeans were well ensconced. They busied themselves helping mushers and filled their free time learning to play cribbage. They spoke English very well, were always friendly and helped make Takotna a comfortable place tough to leave, especially with temperatures plunging toward 50 degrees below zero outside the warm community center. Yet there was no choice for mushers but to forge off toward the great nothingness.

The trail through the Innoko River country between

Takotna and Ruby starts off pleasant enough, climbing over smooth snow on the old road to Ophir and then dropping down toward the Innoko River, crossing road bridges on a few creeks and finally arriving at Dick Forsgren's old cabin. Forsgren, like Dick Newton, was long a mainstay in these parts. A fighter pilot in World War II and Korea, he first came to Alaska in 1956 to work for the Civilian Aviation Agency in Galena. He went from the CAA, later the Federal Aviation Administration, to FAA jobs in Cordova, Cape Yakataga and finally McGrath, where he settled in. He eventually became mayor of McGrath, acquired a cabin built in the 1930s at nearby Ophir, and came to love the area. He did his moose hunting in Ophir, and for years – until ill health prevented it – helped pack in the Iditarod trail to the north by snowmachine. A one-time member of the Iditarod Trail board of directors, he died in Palmer shortly after the end of the 2010 race.

It is unclear what will become of the cabin he donated years ago for use as the Iditarod checkpoint. It is one of the better structures in the fading ghost town of Ophir. Past Forsgren's cabin, there are only a few still standing buildings before the trail passes along the old airstrip and starts toward the nowhere tent camp now called Cripple. The late Don Bowers, a musher and pilot who wrote the definitive Iditarod Trail guide, described "the trip from here to Cripple and on to Ruby (as) arguably the longest, emptiest, loneliest stretch of trail on the race." He might have understated things.

The trail thump, thump, thumps north over moguls interrupted only by big ka-thumps when it drops off three-foot tall lips at the edges of frozen, snow-covered ponds and creeks. Much of the countryside is covered with black spruce so thin and scraggly it can't really be called forest, but something more like tundra with a sprinkling of miniature trees that look to be dying. They only add to the sense of foreboding. The occasional creek bottom, where trees do grow, comes as a welcome change of scenery. Veteran mushers, who know the country, will often take advantage of these thin bands of vegetation as places to camp, maybe build a fire, and give their team a break on a long trail that seems to grow longer even as one moves along it.

The Iditarod's official guide puts the distance from Ophir to Cripple at 62 miles, but it's wrong. Bowers, in 2000, estimated the distance at closer to 105 miles, but the checkpoint that year was at the deserted mining camp of Poorman, 20 miles or so past Cripple. Various sources, citing GPS tracking data, now put the mileage to Cripple in the range of 75 to 80. Nearly all sources do agree the new Cripple checkpoint adjacent to Wolf Kill Lake has been at least 20 miles past the mapped Cripple checkpoint for a decade. Needless to say, Cripple is far enough from Ophir that mushers need to stop and feed their teams along the way, and the seemingly endless run makes it easy to start thinking you somehow overshot the turn off the main Iditarod Trail, to the temporary collection of tents and WeatherPORTs that comprise the checkpoint.

Kotzebue's John Baker drew this conclusion in 2010. He was leading the race at the time, and his hours-long stop only about four miles short of Cripple might well have cost him the win. Tim Hewitt, a hiker who has several times joined the Iditarod Trail Invitational to walk the trail to Nome, met Baker hiking the wrong way on the trail in the dark of night and asked him what he was doing. Baker, Hewitt remembered, said he was looking for the Iditarod

Trail. Hewitt told the musher he was on it. Baker, somewhat to the amazement of the Pennsylvania barrister hiking north, wouldn't believe it. The musher had convinced himself he had gotten off on the wrong trail, gone past the Cripple checkpoint and best stop. He camped outside of Cripple until passed by Dallas Seavey from Seward, who'd left Ophir five hours behind the lead.

Prizes are given along the Iditarod at various checkpoints, and Seavey subsequently grabbed a halfway prize of $3,000 in gold nuggets at Cripple. Baker followed him into the checkpoint and steamed about the marking of the trail, which was well marked. Unfortunately, the front-runner never knows for certain this will be the case. He, or she, is at the mercy of the trail breakers who "X" off the main trail with lathe and divert the route west to the checkpoint.

Because of this, running first to Cripple becomes a calculated risk. The crucial trail-marking X of flimsy lathe could be knocked down by a snowmachine before the Iditarod leader gets there, or the driver could doze off while on the runners only to have his team run straight through the lathe and keep going. A musher behind the leader would recognize the latter mistake upon waking and noticing the absence of sled-runner tracks on the trail, but there is no such signal to tell the leader he might have missed a critical turn.

Baker was making a gamble on leading the race to halfway, and he paid a big price. It is easy to wonder what might have been. After a blowup about having his race ruined by the trail to Cripple, Baker regrouped to finish the Iditarod in fifth, only about seven hours behind champ Lance Mackey. It was an impressive performance given that Baker's camp-out along the trail to Cripple resulted in his ending up nine hours behind Mackey when the race hit the Yukon River at Ruby just past halfway.

Without the stop so close to Cripple, which added at least five hours to Baker's 24-hour mandatory rest at that checkpoint, Iditarod 2010 might have turned out differently. Baker had a lead of over an hour on Mackey when their teams pulled into the Takotna checkpoint, where Mackey stopped to do his 24 while Baker pushed on. It is possible that without the unplanned stop short of Cripple, Baker could have reached the Yukon with Mackey or close to him.

Given that Baker was two hours faster than Mackey from Ruby to Nome, the musher from Kotzebue might have to wonder if this should have been his Iditarod to win. But at least he finally made Cripple and pushed on to the Yukon in good shape. Others were not so lucky. Tom Thurston would never reach halfway, and Emil Churchin would finally struggle into Ruby after 24 hours on the trail from Cripple to see his Iditarod dream die.

14

Tom Thurston

Everyone who starts the Iditarod Trail Sled Dog Race has a plan. Nobody makes it 1,000 miles across the Alaska wilderness with a dog team without one. But some mushers have bigger plans than others. Tom Thurston was one of them. He is a hard-working guy who earned success long before he hit the Iditarod start line in Anchorage.

A 1992 graduate of the University of Florida, Thurston joined corporate America just out of school, decided he didn't like it, and eventually took his business degree west to Oak Creek, Colo. There he started Tom Thurston Construction Inc.

"I always wanted to be a carpenter," he said. Thurston turned out to be more than just a carpenter. He took his business training and his carpentry desires and turned them into a successful business. By the start of the new millennium, Thurston Construction was doing well enough that Thurston started looking around for new challenges. He stumbled into sled dogs.

As for many, it started innocently enough. Thurston had grown up in Massachusetts. He liked skiing and winter camping. Not many of his Colorado friends were into the camping part, but his dog was. They started skiing and camping together. It was fun. Thurston began wondering if it might be even more fun to have a team of dogs to haul around all the necessary winter camping gear. So he tried dog sledding.

"That was cool," he said. It was so cool it didn't take long for the contractor to become a musher. Still, he kept the addiction under control at first. He put together a small, recreational team. They went camping together. They had a good time just being out there.

"I ran dogs for five years before I went to a race," Thurston said. When he did go, it was mainly to prove to himself that the dogs he thought were pretty good were indeed pretty good. They were. More than that, though, Thurston found he enjoyed the competition. It wasn't a big step from there to putting together a bunch of dogs and building a real racing team.

Thus was formed Double T Kennel, named for Tom and his wife, Tami, who runs the kennel's day-to-day operation and organizes sled dog tours in tourist-popular Steamboat Springs. Double T Kennel promptly turned to a well-known neighbor in the state next door to improve the quality of its dogs.

"When we first decided to set racing as a goal we decided to not mess around with potential athletes and especially not the free dogs," Tom notes on the company website. "We went to the top producers of traditional Alaskan huskies and those of the hound-crossed-Alaskan huskies.... Currently the entire kennel is out of three males - Peppy, Ricky and Eltoro - all Swingley, and a half dozen females, also all Swingley."

That would be Swingley as in Doug, the four-time

Iditarod champ and the first non-Alaskan to win The Last Great Race. Swingley demonstrated what was possible. Mushers from Outside have been trying to repeat it ever since. Thurston joined their ranks long before he ran his first Iditarod.

College-educated businessman that he was, he put together a long-term, five-step plan to success: Build a solid team. Prove it capable stateside. Run the Iditarod in 2009 to get a look at Alaska and the trail. Make a low-key race of the Iditarod in 2010. And then come back in 2011 ready to contend for the top 10.

Steps one and two worked perfectly. Thurston put together a strong, fast team, and in 2008, he won Montana's Race to the Sky. A 350-mile race from Lincoln to Owl Creek and back, the race through the Rocky Mountains is one of the premier distance events in the Lower 48. Thurston figured he was Iditarod ready, and came north. His rookie run went as well as could be expected. He finished farther back than he might have liked in 44th, but he got a feel for the big event and enjoyed the trail. Thurston later pronounced the adventure "a huge success."

His team had conquered the rough terrain of the Alaska Range and proven itself in the worst of Alaska weather. Both the temperatures and wind had been brutal at times, but all had survived.

"We traveled up the (Yukon) river for 180 miles through temperatures exceeding minus-50 degrees, wind gusts of 40 to 50 mph and complete exposure," he wrote on his website after the race. "The Yukon is merciless and the entire time the wind was in our face. It was a struggle to keep from blowing over and the dogs never flinched," though the musher did experience some second thoughts about the

Iditarod madness.

Immediately afterward, he said, "I swore I'd never do it again, until about six weeks after being home." Time took the edge off the fierceness of the wind and the bitterness of the cold. The beauty of the country, the thrill of battling across it, and the marvelous performance of the dog team crept to the fore. And the plan, well, the plan was still out there:

Complete the course in 2009. Put the team in the top 30 in 2010. Then come back for that try at the top 10 in 2011.

Almost as quick as Thurston went back to work at his regular job as a contractor in 2009, he went back to what had become his second job as Iditarod musher and Iditarod fundraiser. The latter is vital. Racing the Iditarod is pricey. Thurston had to come up with a lot of money, and he did. By the summer after his first Iditarod, he was prepping for his second.

"I spent eight months, and I spent $50,000 to get there," he said.

The plan was going according to plan, although not exactly according to plan. Thurston had wanted to get to Alaska in January 2010 and give the dogs a couple months to adjust before Iditarod. "I really wanted to run the Copper Basin (300 Sled Dog Race)," he said. Mushers from Outside all agree it is good to get to Alaska months before Iditarod. There is no telling what sorts of viruses are floating among dog teams in Alaska any given year. Better to expose your dogs early and let them build up a tolerance than to expose them during Iditarod when the exertion of the race naturally compromises their immune systems.

Unfortunately, Thurston had business affairs that kept

him in Colorado. He didn't get to Anchorage until a week before the Iditarod start. In retrospect, he said, he probably should have noted that and adjusted his race plan, but he didn't.

"We were running a fairly aggressive schedule," he said. "This year I had so much confidence. Maybe I had too much confidence. I was having so much fun."

He let his team charge north from the start, still aiming to be among the Iditarod top 30. They were 32nd into the Finger Lake checkpoint on the south slope of the Alaska Range, 33rd when the race hit Rainy Pass above, and 29th out of Rohn on the far side of the Range from the start.

Then the plan started to fall apart. Some dogs got sick on the long, 75-mile run from Rohn through the Post River country, into the Farewell Lakes and over the Farewell Hills to Nikolai. Thurston stopped and camped for six hours. He thought the dogs might improve with rest. Some did. Others did not. He ended up hauling two into Nikolai in his sled and dropping them there to recover. He gave the team another long rest and left 44th. The dogs still looked pretty ragged 50 miles down the trail in McGrath. Thurston declared his mandatory, 24-hour rest. The dogs slept. He worried. Most of the race went past.

By the time Thurston left McGrath, he was behind the 51st place team. He wasn't overly worried about his position. He reassured himself the strategy going in had been to go easy to the village of Ruby on the Yukon River just beyond halfway before starting to race, and he was still more than 150 miles short of that checkpoint. But he was worried about how lethargic his team looked.

Coming off that long 24-hour rest in McGrath, they went 20 miles to Takotna and then another 25 miles over the 800-foot dome between there and Ophir. When Thurston stopped to rest the team, most of the dogs didn't want to eat. The temperature was 46 degrees below zero. A veterinarian with whom the musher consulted said several of the dogs were running temperatures and appeared to have come down with something. Thurston was in shock.

"Typically in the cold, my dogs eat like wolves," he said. "Only two of them ate. They didn't look good. I thought they looked skinny. In my opinion, they were too thin to make it to Nome. We had to 600 to 700 miles to go."

Thurston sat there in the lone cabin that houses the checkpoint in the deserted gold town of Ophir. The race swirled around him. He talked to veterinarians about what to do. They suggested it might be a good idea to give up. In the end, he did as they suggested. He gave up on his Iditarod dream for the year.

"It just wasn't how I chose to run dogs," Thurston said. "I didn't want to go on like that. I didn't want to compromise the trust they put in me."

He left the sickest dogs in the care of vets, hitched up the healthy ones and turned back for McGrath. It was sort of his own Iditarod farewell tour. "I didn't want to leave," he said.

Thurston and 10 of his dogs had one of their best runs of Iditarod 2010 going the wrong way on the trail back to the south. He was heartbroken at the decision to quit, but managed a smile upon seeing the pace of his team pick up. They had their tails up and their ears erect. They looked to be having fun again.

"These are my best friends," Thurston said there along the trail, motioning to the dogs attached to his sled. "They were born in my living room."

Back in Anchorage later, he was reunited with the rest of his friends. Three weeks on from that, they were all back home together in Oak Creek with Thurston contemplating what to do next. The original Idit-a-plan was in tatters, but he wasn't ready to give up the Iditarod dream just yet.

"I've got to do some fundraising," he said. "I'm giving myself 60 days. I want to go back."

He was wrestling with whether to pick up where he left off with the veteran dogs from 2009, or start all over with a new group of young dogs who'd never known the defeat of 2010. Young dogs would mean going back to step three. His veteran dogs might enable him to follow through on step four – a top-30 finish. He wasn't sure what was the best strategy. The plan that had been so clear only a month earlier wasn't so clear anymore. Thurston was really sure of only one thing.

"I have really good dogs," he said. "They're good dogs. It wasn't their fault."

15

Emil Churchin

As Tom Thurston went back through Takotna, headed in the wrong direction, poet Emil Churchin was packing his sled to head north on the trail to Ruby. Having just completed the one mandatory rest required of all Iditarod teams somewhere along the trail, he was the last musher to leave the Takotna checkpoint on the 170-mile trek to the Yukon River across some of the most desolate and foreboding country in Alaska. Race rules would have allowed him to go just after struggling Canadian Hank DeBruin pulled through, but Churchin limped around on a badly swollen leg getting his dogs ready until Debruin was out of sight down the old road toward the ghost town of Ophir.

Debruin had completed his 24-hour stop back along the trail in McGrath, wondering the whole time what sort of dog team he would have when he left. His dogs had been slow, making only five or six miles per hour, ever since Rainy Pass. Born, raised and trained in the shelter of the forests on the edge of Ontario's Algonquin Park, the dogs had never experienced a ground blizzard. They'd balked at fighting into blowing snow and headwinds gusting to 40 miles per hour as the trail climbed into the Alaska Range, and though they made it through, they'd been in a bit of a funk ever since.

By McGrath, Debruin, a smiling, bearded guy in a red snowsuit who'd have made a good Santa if not so skinny, was beginning to worry he might not make the cut-off deadlines for mushers at the back of the pack.

New rules, designed to simplify race logistics and roll up checkpoints quickly behind the race, required mushers to reach McGrath within 72 hours of the race leaders. They were to be in Galena on the Yukon River within 96 hours. Teams that missed those deadlines faced the possibility of being withdrawn as "not competitive." Debruin hit McGrath less than 41 hours after Jeff King, the first musher to arrive there, but still he worried as he headed down the trail toward Takotna, a checkpoint famous for its hearty meals and Jan Newton's pies.

He did not stop but went on through and kept going for Ophir. The cabin there was its normal busy, crowded, Iditarod self when first Churchin and then Debruin pulled in on the evening of March 12. Coming off that 24-hour rest in Takotna, Churchin had caught and passed Debruin coming over the hill, but the Canadian's Siberian huskies – a breed never known for great speed – had picked up the pace. Their speed averaged better than eight miles per hour. Debruin and Churchin were by then about four hours behind the rest of the Iditarod field, but looked to be doing okay. They were making steady progress, and they were traveling together, which minimized fears about their safety in the bitter cold chilling the trail.

Neither musher lingered long in the Ophir checkpoint, either. They snacked and watered their dogs and were gone in an hour on the trail to Cripple. Churchin's team beat

Debruin's in there as it had into Ophir. The dogs looked good, but the musher wasn't doing so well. The stump that had taken Mike Suprenant out of the race back at Rainy Pass had nailed Churchin, too. It hooked his sled brake and slammed his team to a halt in a split second. The sudden stop sent Churchin hurtling into the sled. He smashed his leg on a stanchion.

It bothered him for days, but he didn't look at it until on break in Takotna. There he found the whole leg swollen and colored an ugly blackish blue. Someone suggested he should wrap it. He circled it with an ace bandage. The elastic wrap was too tight. On the trail between Ophir and Cripple, his leg started throbbing, and he stopped to wrestle the bandage out from beneath his snowsuit at 40 degrees below zero. When he got to Cripple, he was lucky to find the mushing Galleas working as checkers. Jim Gallea is an Iditarod veteran and a doctor in residency finishing his medical training in Maine. His dad, Bill, is a family practice physician in Montana.

"They looked over my leg," Churchin said. "They told me the swelling would go down eventually, and the blood would get absorbed." But the Galleas noted a little a rest wouldn't hurt. So Churchin watched Debruin's team steam off into the cold after 10 hours rest, then he stayed another six. Churchin figured that even if he didn't catch Debruin's slower team on the 70- or 75-mile run to Ruby, he'd get close.

He figured wrong. More problems started for Churchin almost as soon as he walked out the door of the heated tent at Cripple and the roll of steam came in behind him. He was still almost within sight of the checkpoint when his sled slid into a tree and a stanchion broke. He fixed that quickly, but then the dogs started acting up. There was a female in heat in the team, and everyone seemed to want in on the action. Churchin stopped the team repeatedly to move dogs around to keep the female away from males with more interest in her than travel. That just made things worse.

"I was just a bumbling fool," Churchin said. "I stopped too many times. Team discipline broke down."

What should have been at most a 36-hour run between Alaska's two great Interior rivers turned into a two-and-a-half-day trek destined to prove heartbreaking in so many ways. The bad luck that had seemed to haunt Churchin for more than 500 miles north along the trail finally caught him with full force four miles shy of the Yukon. The death of his Iditarod dream began there in the dark on a Sunday night with his team in revolt. Despite the 40-degree-below-zero cold that brutalizes both people and dogs, Churchin decided the only way to restore order was to camp until everyone calmed down. He thought that with a night's rest the dogs would mellow out.

That didn't exactly happen. After a night out, a stiff and half-frozen musher rose on a bitter Monday morning to try to coax a cold and unhappy dog team the last two miles to the top of the final hill outside the old, riverside mining town of Ruby. It was a difficult task despite the sunshine brightening the spruce trees thick atop the rolling hills just back from the mighty river locked in ice. It was a pretty sun, but not a warm one.

Only one dog in Churchin's team appeared ready to charge down the trail into the new day, and it was back in the team – not up in lead. Churchin couldn't find a known leader who wanted to do anything but stand in the cold,

stare at the musher and wonder why. About the only interest the dogs showed in activity centered on that female in
heat. A fair number of Churchin's team wanted to get close
to her again. The musher limped among his gang, moving
this dog to the front, that dog to the back, trying to find
some combination of dogs that would work together to get
the team moving.

His efforts to snap and unsnap dogs were hampered by a
bulky bandage on one hand. The bandage covered the spot
where he'd sliced his palm near to the bone while trying to
cut off an earlier bandage covering a split finger. The limp
was the result of that bad leg banged up early in the race.
The reluctance and confusion in the dog team was the fault
of all the simple rookie mistakes made daily almost from
the beginning of Churchin's Iditarod run.

The rookie musher spent so much time caring for his
dogs that he forgot to care for himself. He forgot to drink
and he let himself get dehydrated. He found it impossible
to sleep and left himself in the stupor of sleep deprivation.
He didn't take care of the injured leg soon enough. All of it
contributed to the fateful decisions before and during the
long push on the trail from Cripple to Ruby.

He should have left the female in heat behind at the
checkpoint. He shouldn't have been stopping and starting
all the time to switch dogs. That sort of thing demoralizes
any team. And most of all he shouldn't have given up and
camped just shy of the top of the last hill before the trail
went all downhill to Ruby.

Had Churchin known how close he was to the top, he
could have taken the lead dogs and walked them over the
crest. But for the bad leg, he could have walked the team all
the way into the village of 150 to 200 people. It was not far,

and it would have been better for everyone than a lengthy camp-out in the bone-numbing cold. But Churchin did not do these things because he did not know. Instead, he did the best he could to make camp. He dug the dogs snow caves. He cut a few spruce boughs to put in the bottoms. He put the dogs in their coats. And he settled in to wait until they were ready to get up and walk over the hill on their own.

"My toes got very cold," he said. "The dogs were shivering all night."

When worried Iditarod race judge Kevin Saiki and Ruby checker Jimmy Honea went out from the village on snowmachines to determine what had been keeping Churchin for almost 24 hours on the run in from Cripple, the musher was still waiting for his team to rouse itself. Saiki told Churchin the time had come to see if he could get the dogs going.

After the Anchorage musher finally got the team lined out, a couple of the dogs at least did seem ready. They were anxious to go, barking and yanking against their harnesses. But most of the dogs just seemed confused, unsure of what Churchin wanted them to do. It took him quite a while, shifting dogs around all the time and finally zipping the problem-causing bitch into the sled bag, before he got the team moving, and even then it was a slow, stop-and-go walk and trot to the top of the hill where the dogs seemed to be suddenly reborn.

Once over the crest, they took off, loping down the slope, roaring around a corner on the road into the village, and charging up the hill and into the Ruby checkpoint. Churchin, whose spirits had been darker than the night only hours before, seemed buoyed by their performance. But any optimism he mustered was destined to die shortly after a phone conversation with Iditarod race marshal Mark Nordman. The conversation in the Ruby community center was conducted in private, but it was clear what Churchin was told. He was so far behind the rest of the mushers in the race – more than half a day behind even Debruin now – that he had two choices: He could scratch on his own, or he could be withdrawn.

"That left me no choice," Churchin said. He signed a form saying he was scratching, and then the tears flowed and flowed. He could not stem them no matter how hard he tried.

"Two years of my life and all of my money," he said. "This is where I was going to turn my life around, and I failed. Every step of the way I knew everything I did wrong, and I did it again and again. It is the story of my life."

It is not, actually, the story of Churchin's life. He is a 42-year-old man with a digital imaging job on the North Slope. By all modern standards, he is successful. He earns a good living.

"I'm making the best money I ever made," he admitted. "That's how I fund this. God, I could have built a house with all the money I spent on this. I maxed out my credit cards. If I had finished, I could have had some post-race fundraisers."

Now, he said, "I think about all the people that donated. I got several thousand dollars from family and friends."

He felt he'd let them all down. He was in a dark place. He was supposed to have made it to Nome. He was supposed to have shown he could do what so few ever accomplish.

He was supposed to have lived the dream that began not long after Iditarod veteran Jim Lanier from Chugach introduced Churchin to sled dogs.

Churchin bought into the dream with everything – heart, soul and bankroll. It was painful beyond belief when the dream came crashing down.

"I need to stop blubbering," he told Saiki, but he could not. The sense of grief was so deep.

Everyone in the checkpoint tried to console him that it was better to have tried and come up short than never to have tried at all. Churchin was buying none of it. In time, he would, but in the moment, he could not.

"The year I worked with Jim Lanier, he broke his foot on day two of the race, and he finished 40th," Churchin said. "I think Jim Lanier is going to be embarrassed to be associated with me. Any other musher would have this team in the top 30. This won't be a good memory. I wanted that (finisher's) belt buckle."

He was sure there would never be another chance to go to Nome. The Iditarod is too expensive, he said; the training too time-consuming, his bungling such that no competent musher would ever want to work with him.

"If you look at my race, it's all there," he said. "It's just a prime example of how not to run the race."

Saiki put a hand on the musher's shoulder.

"We're gonna go to McGrath, get you washed up, talk," Saiki said. Things would be better, Saiki promised. He explained how he, too, had scratched from an Iditarod, and he had survived. Churchin wiped more tears from his eyes.

Far north on the trail, past Iditarod champions Lance Mackey and Jeff King were closing on Nome. They made the Iditarod look so easy.

"I have a new-found respect," Churchin said. "How can Jeff King and Lance Mackey be so far ahead? I don't know how they do it."

Then he put his head in his hand and cried some more. It was hard to wrestle with how a race so seemingly simple could become suddenly impossible. It took some time for the emotional wounds to begin to heal, but eventually they did. Friends welcomed Churchin home. A group of them got into his apartment and posted notes of encouragement everywhere.

"That cheered me up," he said after the Iditarod ended. "In the bedroom, the note said, 'Welcome to the warm.' When I opened my laptop, there was a big one in there that said, 'Failure is never risking the attempt.'"

Churchin risked the attempt. He's proud of that, but he still broods over the abrupt finish to his race and his exhausted coffers. His race gutted the bank account, drained the charity of his friends and pushed him into debt. Had he made it to Nome, the financial sacrifices would have all been worth it – more than worth it. But now he can only wish for what might have been, what could have been, what he believes should have been.

16

Ruby to Unalakleet

The good thing about the northern route of the Iditarod Trail is that things usually get better for mushers at Ruby. After the 170-mile crossing from Ophir through the foreboding black spruce barrens, past the ghost town camps and abandoned equipment from the old mining days, through the wildfire blackened barrens around deserted Poorman, and below the crumbling suspension bridge to nowhere connecting roads that barely exist anymore at Sulatana Crossing, it's nice to reach a community still alive.

Ruby isn't what it once was – there were 3,000 people here in 1911 in a booming Yukon River port at the end of a system of roads that went 100 miles south into the hills to service the gold mines – but the 180 remaining residents pull together to provide a warm welcome for mushers at the old, log community hall in the center of town. And the dog drivers can look forward to much better trail heading west.

Once down past the rocky bluff just outside of the village, it is only 50 miles on to the next Iditarod checkpoint at Galena, once the forward operating base for U.S. Air Force fighter jets guarding Alaska's western border with what is now Russia. From Galena, it is but another 40 miles to Nulato, an ancient trading center. Long before the first white men arrived there, the Athabascan Indians from the Interior were doing business with the Inupiat Eskimos from the coast. The first white traders – Russians – didn't show up until 1839 to open a post. The post was wiped out in the Nulato massacre of 1851. Historical accounts are unclear as to exactly what happened, but indications are a battle might have broken out in a dispute over local trade. Most of the dead – 53 – were Nulato Natives killed by Koyukuk River Natives, according to most accounts, but the Russian post manager and a British naval officer who happened to be visiting the village were also reported among the dead.

Much has changed since the mid-1800s. Today, Nulato – like Ruby – is a community that welcomes the Iditarod with open arms as does Kaltag, another village 50 miles downriver at the start of the Kaltag Portage to the Bering Sea coast. For mushers, the spacing of these villages along the river makes life so much easier because they are freed the burden of carrying a sled-full of extra dog food and spared the hassle of melting snow to make water for broth for the dogs. They can run with checkpoint-to-checkpoint convenience from Ruby to Galena to Nulato to Kaltag.

Beyond Kaltag, it is a 90-mile jump to Unalakleet on the Bering Sea coast, but the U.S. Bureau of Land Management provides two snug and comfortable log cabins along the Iditarod Trail over the portage. The Tripod Flats cabin is about 35 miles out of Kaltag, the Old Woman cabin another 15 miles on. Some mushers choose to grab food and straw in Kaltag and push on through that checkpoint on a long run all the way from Nulato to Tripod Flats cabin. Others take a break at Kaltag, and then haul food and straw to Old Woman for another stop there.

Sitting in a clearing in a stand of spruce below Old Woman Mountain, the cabin is in another of those iconically beautiful spots along the Iditarod Trail. Iditarod champ Susan Butcher asked that after her death her ashes be scattered atop the mountain. They now look down on the race from there.

The run along the Yukon River and then over the Kaltag Portage to Unalakleet is supposed to be one of the easier in the race. The trail between the river villages is regularly traveled all winter, and thus it is solidly packed and well marked. Not only that, but the winds that historically tear at the faces of mushers and dogs on the Iditarod's southern route up the river from Anvik to Kaltag, are usually at everyone's back on the northern route.

Unfortunately for some of the dog teams and their drivers, Mother Nature changed the rules for 2010. She sent a cold, nasty wind whistling upriver from Kaltag. Mushers and dogs sometimes battled into wind chill temperatures pushing 70 to 80 degrees below zero. It was enough for three teams. Forty-six-year-old Judy Currier, already suffering with an aching back, decided to bail out at Galena. She was joined by 27-year-old Ryan Redington from Wasilla, a grandson of race founder Joe Redington Sr., and 34-year-old Warren Palfrey from Quesnel, British Columbia,

Canada. Redington and Palfrey had hoped to contend for Iditarod honors. When they decided that wasn't going to happen, they figured it best to load themselves and their dogs in an airplane and fly home.

Others struggled on, hoping for the weather to break, hoping things would get better as the race neared the coast.

"The cold mentalled out my dogs," said Soldotna's Jane Faulkner. "I can't get anyone to run in swing. At this point, I'm just following Celeste [Davis]." The two nurses were, by then partners on the trail, the slow but steady dogs of Montanan Davis leading Faulkner's pampered pets onward. Davis' nose was still swollen and her eyes black from the collision with the stump in the Dalzell Gorge. Faulkner's hands were blistered and badly swollen from frostbite. "I didn't take into consideration how much my hands would swell," she said. But no matter how badly beaten up, they were headed for the coast.

Just ahead of them was Canadian Ross Adam, a sea-soned veteran musher on a camping trip north with a team of young dogs. He was getting almost eight hours sleep in every checkpoint and enjoying himself despite the cold. Still, he was exultant as the race moved away from the Interior toward the coast and the thermometer began to climb upward from 45 degrees below zero to 30 degrees below to near 25 degrees below.

"I'm so excited about this warm weather," Adam said. "Last night the dogs weren't shivering. They sort of settled down and started to relax for the first time. Even out there now, as cold as it is (at minus 27), it's totally different from what it was."

The temperature, to be exact, was almost twice as warm

as in the Innoko country as Adam, Davis and Faulkner made their way to the coast. Behind them only one man and one team – Canadian Hank Debruin and his Siberian huskies – were still struggling through the icebox of the Interior.

17

Hank Debruin

When Emil Churchin's Iditarod dream died, Hank Debruin's Iditarod dream was put in jeopardy. The Iditarod does not like to leave a lone dog team hanging far behind the pack. This is as much or more about the dogs and race logistics as about the people.

To begin to understand why, you must visualize how the Iditarod race looks something like an overfed snake as it moves up the trail. There are a few teams at the front, a few teams at the back, and a big gut full of teams in the middle. The volunteer Iditarod Air Force focuses its efforts near the gut. It is busy all the time moving people and gear up and down the trail and thus remains available, if the need arises, to aid in rescues.

After Pat Moon hit a tree and knocked himself out of Iditarod 2010, the Air Force was on the scene quickly to load him in an airplane and fly him to a hospital. Moon was still near the middle of the pack when this happened. That made rescue easier than if he had been off the back, and the farther off the back a team goes, the harder it gets for the Air Force, or other Iditarod officials, to respond to a crisis in a timely manner.

The consequences of this were spelled out in deadly detail in Iditarod 2009 as back-of-the-pack mushers struggled on the race's southern route across the desolate country between Ophir and the tiny village of Shageluk on the Innoko River. This is a corner of Alaska every bit as foreboding and empty as the country between Ophir and Ruby, if not more so. And it was here the Iditarod's near worst-case scenario unfolded.

The last three mushers to leave the Iditarod checkpoint set up in the ghost town of Iditarod marched out into a raging hell of a storm. Two of them – Kim Darst from New Jersey and Blake Matray from Two River – were traveling together. Darst was an Iditarod rookie. Officially, Matray was, too, but he'd run part of the 2003 Iditarod when the race was for the first and only time begun in the Interior community of Nenana because of low snow in the Alaska Range. He didn't make it to Nome that year, but he learned a lot.

Matray had more than just this limited Iditarod Trail experience going for him, too. A graduate of the U.S. Air Force Academy, he'd been thoroughly trained in outdoor survival, and he'd spent a lot of time in-country in Alaska. Since 1990, when he took a job with the Alaska Air National Guard, he'd been living with and running dogs in the Interior where 40- to 50-degree-below-zero cold becomes, whether one likes it or not, something of a norm.

Almost 11 hours in front of Matray and Darst, but traveling alone, was Wasilla doctor Lou Packer. He was, almost everyone agreed, an all around good guy who'd spent 22 years in the 49th state. But like most Alaskans in the 21st century, his had been a largely urban life. Born in California, raised in Los Angeles, a product of UCLA and the University of California-Berkeley, Packer really hadn't started to immerse himself in the Alaska beyond the road system until 2006, and his pre-Iditarod adventures had yet to take him deep into the Alaska wild.

To qualify for the Iditarod, he ran a couple relatively easy mid-distance races in the Susitna Valley. He had experienced some tough trail and some bad weather, but nothing like what he was to experience on the trail to Shageluk. Packer's team pushed out over the incessant hills that stack up on either side of the Little Yentna and Big Yentna rivers and into a killer blizzard.

It caught them in all its ferocity on an exposed ridge. The team stalled. The sideways blowing snow filled and obliterated the trail, the trail that held the only snow packed firm enough to support dogs. Off the trail, the dogs sank so deep in white fluff they had to swim. Packer went in up to his chest. The contrast between the trail and the snow to either side made it easy to tell when off trail, but getting back on trail was laborious work.

The musher and the dogs lost the trail, found it again with their feet, then lost it. The process was repeated again and again until Packer decided it was senseless to try go forward, or to go back. He and the team would exhaust themselves trying to find the trail and get almost nowhere. The musher decided the best and only option was to camp, though he feared it might be the last camp he ever made.

"I was in big trouble at that point," Packer said. "I was worried I was going to freeze to death."

The temperature had dropped to 45 degrees below zero. The winds, Packer said, felt like "a semi tractor-trailer passing you at 80 miles an hour." He dug his dogs into snow caves as best he could. Then he got inside his sled bag, zipped himself into his sleeping bag, and hoped he'd live to see another day.

He did. Two of his dogs didn't. They froze to death. The Iditarod suddenly faced a crisis. The death of two dogs overshadowed everything else that had happened in the killer storm of 2009. Ignored by the world were the residents of the tiny village of Shageluk who risked their lives to set out on the trail to find struggling mushers and teams. Overlooked were the heroics of dog-cuddling mushers Matray and Darst, who managed to save another hypothermic husky on the verge of death. Forgotten were the volunteers of the Iditarod Air Force who eventually arrived on the scene like a winged cavalry to evacuate everyone and ensure no more dogs, or people, died in the storm. All that mattered was that dogs had died.

Outcries started immediately. The Associated Press wrote a story about Packer that gave People for the Ethical Treatment of Animals (PETA) spokeswoman Desiree Acholla a platform to claim the Iditarod was racing dogs to their death even if Packer, a back-of-the-pack musher toiling north along the trail never went fast enough to actually be considered in a race at all. Tim Dahlberg, a national columnist for the Associated Press, picked up the PETA theme and jumped in to claim Alaskans "don't have a problem with chaining up big packs of dogs and running them to within an inch of their life for sport."

Dahlberg, of course, had never seen the Iditarod. If he had, he might have known that the dogs aren't chained together, and that the quickest way to end an Iditarod run is to ask the dogs to run "to within an inch of their life." Ask them to do that, and they will quit. They might quit anyway for any number of reasons, including the simple breakdown in team discipline Emil Churchin encountered.

But Dahlberg's lack of knowledge as to the relationships between mushers and their teams, let alone how the Iditarod works, didn't stop his nationally syndicated column from lending credibility to those who consider the Iditarod cruel or inhumane or both. Most of them, like Dahlberg, had never witnessed the race, but that didn't matter either.

Led by a woman in Florida who once visited an Alaska dog lot and thought dogs shouldn't be forced to spend any parts of their lives on chains outside of a doghouse, they began peppering Iditarod sponsors with demands to drop their sponsorships. And Iditarod organizers, always worried about bad press, worried as they had worried for at least 20 years.

Nobody liked to see a dog die. It was as painful for the musher to whom it happened as it was for any loving pet owner, and it was painful for race supporters. Sometimes dogs just up and died for reasons hard to discern, but if there were dogs dying from preventable causes, everyone agreed, the problem should be fixed.

After the deaths of Packer's dogs, there was a lot of discussion, some public and some private, about how to avoid another "Packer" incident. Rules were changed to more thoroughly screen mushers before allowing them to run Iditarod. Rookies were required to accumulate at least 500 miles of sled dog travel in mid-distance races, find a veteran musher to sponsor their entry into the big race, and then convince a "qualifying board" of their competence. The qualifying board was to get report cards from organizers of mid-distance qualifying races with which to substantiate whether a rookie was qualified.

A couple mushers already entered in Iditarod 2010 had problems with the new qualifying board. They were told to run extra races and gain more experience. They did.

Not that anyone versed in Iditarod had all that much faith that this new system would be all that much better than that of the past, which required only that mushers and their teams survive the qualifying races. The fact was, and is, that the Bushcraft among Iditarod mushers varies greatly. Some running their first race are as comfortable in the immensity of the Alaska wilderness as any old sourdough. And some who have run more than a few races can sometimes still be intimidated by a wilderness that appears to stretch on to eternity, and weather that, Dear God, sometimes seems to want to kill a man or a woman.

Legendary Iditarod champ Susan Butcher, a woman who feared no one, was once scared enough of the weather to turn back to the safety of a checkpoint. So, too, for two of the men who followed the late, great Iditarod star out onto the trail from White Mountain to Nome near the end of the 1991 race. And yet there were two others – soon-to-be five-time champ Rick Swenson from Two Rivers and later four-time champ Martin Buser from Big Lake – who though pounded by the weather felt confident they and their teams could safely press through to Nome. And they did.

They were fine, and their dogs were fine, although the blowing snow and the wind were so bad that a worried Swenson at one point put his thickest coated dogs in coats on the windward side of his team to protect his thinner coated dogs from the worst of blow. How much the dogs appreciated that will never be known, but Swenson's team reached Nome in good shape to win the '91 Iditarod.

Had Hank Debruin been Rick Swenson or Martin Buser, there would have been no concern on anyone's part about his trailing behind the Iditarod pack as the race came up the Yukon. Had not Packer lost two dogs to hypothermia in that storm in 2009, there might have been a lot less concern about Debruin coming up the river alone.

Almost from the beginning, the friendly Canadian and his Siberian huskies – Slow-berians as serious racers were prone to call them – had been near the back of the Iditarod. The 45th team to leave the race's restart in Willow, they worked steadily backward to 47th at Yentna Station, 51st at Skwentna, 62nd at Finger Lake and, finally, 68th at Rainy Pass.

It didn't bother Debruin. He was comfortable out there alone at the back of the Iditarod field. He had a 13-day schedule for completing the race, and he was sticking to it. He was enjoying the trail and his Joe Redington-Jack London-Sgt. Preston vision of it. He really didn't care what other mushers did.

When a bunch of them decided to hold in Rainy Pass because of weather, he went ahead and jumped up to the 59th spot in the race, even though his team had to struggle through a scary new environment. The team had never experienced the kind of winds they encountered in the Alaska Range. They were reluctant to march into the blowing snow that stung at their eyes and the whipping winds that pinned their ears against their heads. For days afterward, Debruin would note the dogs remained in a bit of a funk. A solid but plodding bunch in the best of times, they

were slowed more by bad attitude. Fifty-ninth out of Rohn, Debruin's team was back down to 62nd and second-to-last by Nikolai, 75 miles on along the trail. By McGrath, as the teams behind starting dropping out one by one, Debruin was back to 62nd and last.

He was starting to worry then about the Iditarod's new time rules. Those, too, were fallout from the 2009 race. Rob Loveman, a physicist from Colorado, was pulled from the 2009 event for lack of competitiveness. Loveman had never expected to be competitive in the sense of vying for position in the Iditarod. He even confessed to being a bit of bumbler on the trail. But, he argued, he was competent to take care of dogs in the wilderness, and he was engaged in his own personal competition to simply make it to the finish in Nome. Loveman took his withdrawal hard.

"What became clear to me was that the race marshal had decided to pull me from the race before he had spoken to me," he later wrote. "He didn't ask a single question that would tell him whether or not I might be capable of dealing with the weather he knew would be moving in. I asked to be able to make the run between Ophir and Iditarod and the race marshal simply said I had a choice between scratching at Ophir and being withdrawn for not being competitive. I certainly wasn't scratching. I chose to be withdrawn. The dogs were doing well. I felt good about that and good about not scratching. As long as I can safely put one foot in front of another, I'll move forward. Prior to the race, I believed that as long as I could do that, I could get to Nome and get my belt buckle. Having that opportunity taken from me stung."

Race Marshall Nordman saw his Iditarod exchange with

Loveman differently. He thought the two men had agreed it would be in the best interest of everyone – Loveman, Loveman's dogs and the race – for the Coloradan to quit. Nordman's view of their conversation only stung Loveman more. He appealed Nordman's decision. Loveman asked that the withdrawal be overturned, that his entry fee be refunded and donated to an animal rescue organization, that the Iditarod apologize, and that his journey to Ophir be credited as one of his mid-distance qualifying races for Iditarod 2010.

The Iditarod board of directors voted without comment to uphold the withdrawal. Loveman sued. One of the key arguments in his suit [pending as the 2010 race began] was that the race rule dictated a musher was "out of the competition," if he or she was "no longer making a valid effort to compete.'" He noted the race rules contained no provision for withdrawing a team based solely on speed along the trail. Though the Iditarod contested Loveman's lawsuit, essentially arguing that it was not bound by the same race rules as the mushers, it did rewrite Rule 36, the so-called "competitiveness rule," for 2010 to comply with at least two of Loveman's legal arguments. The wording on competition was changed, and time limits were added. The new rule said this:

> *"A team may be withdrawn that is out of the competition and is not in position to make a valid effort to compete. If a team has not reached McGrath in 72 hours of the leader, Galena within 96 hours of the leader or, Unalakleet within 120 hours of the leader, it may be presumed that a team is not competitive. A musher whose conduct constitutes an unreasonable risk of harm to his/*

her dogs or other persons may also be withdrawn."

The timelines worried Debruin, but he was well within them. He hit McGrath with more than 40 hours to spare. He was in Galena more than 24 hours before the cutoff. And then came Nulato, a friendly village of about 300 that opened the Andrew K. Demoski School to welcome mushers. The Iditarod was rolling up the checkpoint there when Debruin arrived. A pair of race volunteers from Outside, who'd flown in to keep an accurate account of race times, were hurrying to catch an airplane out of town as were the two Austrian vets who'd worked the checkpoint. They did check Debruin's Siberian huskies, and said the dogs looked fine.

Debruin himself was in good spirits "Nice run, nice night," he said when he arrived with icicles hanging from his beard. He fed and watered his dogs and planned to give them a long rest before pushing all the way to the Old Woman cabin on the Kaltag Portage before making the next long stop.

Told during his rest stop that Mackey had just won the race to Nome, hundreds of miles ahead, the 39-year-old Canadian could only express wonderment.

"It's amazing, aye," he said. "I wish I could trade him teams for a day."

The driver of Slow-berians wondered what it would like to ride behind a truly speedy team, but he was enjoying his dogs. They all rested well outside the Nulato school as the temperature started to climb toward zero. Debruin, who confessed then that he never had been able get warm battling into a headwind on the river during the night, took a nap in the warm school. Finally, as late afternoon slipped toward evening, he made ready to leave.

He was back outside putting booties on the dogs and enjoying the 10-or 15-degree-below temperatures, which were three times warmer than anything anyone had seen in days, when he got a phone call from Race Marshall Nordman, who was in Nome where Mackey had already won the race. Debruin was in Nulato by himself. There was no race official there to help sort things out as there had been with Kevin Saiki in Ruby when Churchin scratched. Only two people will ever know what was said on the phone, if even they know.

Nordman has the toughest job in the Iditarod race. He is charged with both keeping the race moving and keeping everyone safe – dogs, mushers, pilots, volunteers and vets. He could not have helped but be troubled by the fact that Debruin's team was again down to five miles per hour between Galena and Ruby on the Yukon. It's a long, long way from Nulato to Nome at that speed. Fat-tired bikes ridden by competitors in the Iditarod Trail Invitational – a human-powered race instead of a dog-powered race – are faster. Nordman clearly could not have been happy about Debruin's speed, but whether he told Debruin to get moving or simply queried him to find out whether there was a problem is unclear. Nordman has said he didn't mean to force Debruin to quit. Debruin, a soft- and well-spoken man, after the race wrote a long and eloquent account of his recollections of their conversation for his Facebook page on the internet. It spread as much fog as it spread light.

He was minutes away from leaving Nulato, he wrote, when an Iditarod volunteer approached and "avoiding looking me in the eye said Mark wanted to talk to me before I left. My heart sunk, I couldn't imagine this would be a pleasant conversation. Apparently (friend) Ward and (wife) Tanya's sources had been correct. I should have left sooner. In hindsight I should never have answered the call, should have pulled the hook and left at that moment and I would still likely be on the trail, but when you don't sleep for more than a few hours for days on end, your brain doesn't think as clear as normal so I went in.

"It should be noted that before that moment Mark Nordman had been incredibly kind to both Tanya and I from the signup to the rookie meeting to our 24 in McGrath for which we were and are grateful. The phone call that ensued questioned why the team had run so slow into Nulato and (Nordman) told me I was the slowest team in 15 years to do that stretch. I tried explaining about the cold, the wind, this being new for my dogs, but they did it. I tried saying we had the wind at our back now and would make much better time, how we were going through Kaltag and would be caught up with the back two teams by (Unalakleet), that we were still well within the mandatory cut off times, but nothing I said received any encouragement. I was left with the opinion that I either pull the plug in Nulato or run to Kaltag and have this conversation all over again with the same outcome. If it was to end in 30 miles anyway, I saw no point in asking my dogs to keep going. And with that with no time to reconsider or to call home for perspective, the dream, the time and the investment all seemed for naught.

"I was certainly aware of the new cutoff times and had planned to run a 13-day Iditarod with even run even rest and said that to anyone who asked, and everyone told me that would be fine, I would get there. It was no secret my run was going as planned leaving me lots of buffer time against the new cutoff times, but I guess that wasn't enough. I was on my own. We had fallen behind after our tough run from Nikolai where, like Tom Thurston, I was rotating how many dogs were riding in the sled. Then came the 24 so I was still behind five to six hours, and that can't be caught up in a day but we should have caught the next teams within that day."

Whether Debruin would have caught those teams ahead is debatable. But he'd told Jane Faulkner and Celeste Davis to expect him at the Old Woman cabin on the Kaltag Portage where they planned to take a long, long break – and did – before heading on to Unalakleet on the coast. The trio had hung out enough along the trail that a friendship of sorts had formed.

Davis and Faulkner had been in Cripple to welcome Debruin to the halfway point and offer reassurances.

"How's it going?" Faulkner asked.

"Good," Debruin said.

"I'm glad to see you," Davis added.

"It's a really long way," Debruin said. Davis patted him on the arm. Debruin joked about how his wife, wishing to be helpful, had jotted him trail notes. They made the tough trail to Cripple to be "59 miles" of "fairly flat, rolling wooden hills."

The hills weren't wooded. The trail wasn't flat, more like pound-a-sled-to-pieces rough. And the distance was so far beyond 59 miles it seemed like forever.

"You've got to tell her, 'Honey, you're a little off. I know you meant well,'" Davis joked. Everyone laughed.

"Where were you guys the other night when it hit minus 50," Debruin asked. "I got in my sleeping bag (to rest) and I couldn't feel my toes. I had to walk up and down the trail for three hours to stay warm." The dogs took their scheduled four-hour nap.

"I'm sick of that," Davis said.

Everyone was sick of it as the race moved across the Interior, but the cold was gone by the time Davis and Faulkner reached Old Woman. Their dogs rested there in comparative warmth, the thermometer creeping up toward the freezing point, while the two women wondered what had happened to Debruin back down the trail.

His team was, indeed, slow. But, as it turned out, it wasn't the slowest in 15 years from Galena to Nulato. That honor belonged to Wayne Curtis from Wasilla, who won the dubious distinction in 2008. Curtis, like Debruin, was running Siberians. Curtis, unlike Debruin, went on to finish the 2008 race in a time of 13 days, 23 hours and 25 minutes – almost a day slower than Debruin's unmet 13-day goal for 2010.

Davis and Faulkner had half expected to see Debruin joining them at the Old Woman cabin, but were told as they went through Kaltag that he had quit. Hours later when they stopped to rest at Old Woman, they were wondering why. They'd thought his team looked fine in Nulato. They were sorry to see him gone.

"He's such a nice guy," Davis said before trying to stem the funk with some gallows humor: "But every time someone scratches we move up!"

"I didn't think I was going to make it to Unalakleet," Faulkner added in sympathy with Debruin's plight.

Faulkner would eventually make Unalakleet on the

coast. So would Debruin, but he would arrive angry and frustrated on an Iditarod airplane still trying to sort out how exactly events had transpired to kill his long-held Iditarod dream.

"I'm mad as hell," he said as he waited at the airport to be flown back to Anchorage. Time would take the edge off the anger, but the hurt would remain.

"For over the past decade Iditarod has consumed our dreams and focus," he wrote in that Facebook posting. "While the race certainly didn't end the way we had envisioned, and there will be no celebration in Nome for our team and family, it was an amazing journey. People ask if I will come back and run Iditarod again. Two days ago, I said never. Now I don't know. Without major corporate sponsors most people can't afford to do this race every year. It took us three years to save and fund raise ($50,000) to get here. Maybe if the ITC clarified their rules so they weren't random we might someday...."

Debruin believes Iditarod officials drove a stake through the heart of his dream, and yet he cannot let go. All of this is, in some ways, in keeping with the spirit of what Joe Redington envisioned the Iditarod to be, a challenge not so much of speed – there are plenty of sprint races for that – but of determination and tenacity. Dare to fail! And, if the worst happens, get up, shake it off and dare to try again.

18

Unalakleet to White Mountain

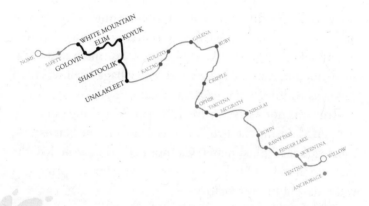

The great dramas of Iditarod's past have all played out along the Bering Sea coast. A major storm was brewing when Libby Riddles arrived in Unalakleet in 1985 on the way to a breakthrough Iditarod victory. She might have stopped in the coastal-hub village, but didn't. Instead she took off to the north down the slough behind the airport runway, out across the tundra and into the willows that partially shield the trail as it starts climbing toward coastal bluffs.

She would find some protection from the wind there in the groves of spruce cut by a snowmachine track that works its way up and down toward a 1,000-foot high crossing of the Blueberry Hills and a three-mile drop to the coastal beach outside of Shaktoolik. But it was not an easy run for the woman who then called the remote Seward Peninsula village of Teller her home. There were long, open patches of tundra swept by the winds, and the ridge tops were hell. The winds screamed like a banshee and the snow blew sideways.

Once back down along the coastal beaches, there was a better than 10-mile run to Shaktoolik through a maelstrom of blowing snow on what is essentially a huge, frozen, inland lake behind the coastal dunes. So much snow was suspended in the gale force winds the village itself was hard to see as Riddles' team worked toward it.

This was not a first for the Iditarod. Much the same had happened during the 1982 race. The late Herbie Nayokpuk, the legendary Shishmaref Cannonball, that year led the race north out of Shaktoolik into windswept emptiness. It was a daring bid for victory.

Between Shaktoolik and Koyuk 50 miles away on the north side of Norton Bay, there is almost nothing. On a clear day, Island Point – a 100-foot tall rock outcropping about five miles out of Shaktoolik – is visible across the treeless, brush-free tundra. It was lost in blowing snow when Nayokpuk left Shaktoolik. Beyond the point there was nothing but Norton Bay ice. There is a cabin, if it can be found, near the point where mushers sometimes hole up in a storm. But Nayokpuk was past the cabin in '82 when the full thrust of near-hurricane force winds stopped his team. He ended up pinned down on the Norton Bay ice for hours. He was eventually forced to retreat to Shaktoolik to survive. Half-frozen, he came into that checkpoint and scratched. His bold bid to win an Iditarod had failed. He never would claim an Iditarod victory, though he would be in the hunt again and again.

Riddles was luckier in 1985. She went out into a storm almost as bad as that which stopped Nayokpuk, but this time the winds did not intensify. She made it across the bay to Koyuk. The move sealed her first and only victory. When she left Koyuk back out onto the sea ice headed for the trail that cuts through the patches of brush and stands of forest on the peninsula behind Bald Head to the southwest, two teams behind her were closing fast, but they would never catch up. Riddles' dogs ran steady across the Kwik River, over the ice of Kwiniuk Inlet, and along the 10-mile spit near Moses Point that leads to an unplowed state highway that climbs through a thick coastal forest before dropping into the village of Elim.

She had a comfortable lead there and went on to become the first woman to win the Iditarod. The 1,000-foot hill mushers call "Little McKinley" still remained to be crossed between Elim and Golovin, but it would not play any real role in her historic Iditarod run.

It was different in 2010, though. The mountain would help to end the Iditarod for Scotsman John Stewart in a year when the Bering Sea coast was as friendly as it could be to the mushers at the back of the Iditarod pack.

There was a breeze blowing across the Blueberry Hills when the last mushers left Unalakleet, but it was neither particularly cold nor particularly strong, and the trail from Shaktoolik to Koyuk crossed what could only be described as a great, windless, sun-washed plain to Koyuk. From there to Elim, the trail did go a little soft in places, which made slightly more work for the dogs, and the temperature climbed enough there were puddles of meltwater forming in that village. Most of the mushers agreed it was probably by then a little too warm for the dogs, but after the bitter cold of the Interior the warmth seemed almost as much of a relief to them as to the people. The team that Jane Faulkner had found reluctant to go on the frozen Yukon kept trying to run away from the team of sidekick Celeste Davis as the nurses left Elim past the cliffs of limestone and dolomite headed west toward Walla Walla and the start of the climb up and over Little McKinley.

They were, by then, closing on the young Scotsman Stewart who'd once been far to the front but had been struggling and dropping back farther and farther day by day. His team labored over Little McKinley in the heat of the day, slogged along the snow-covered ice of Golovin Bay, trudged through the center of the tiny village of Golovin, and finally struggled toward White Mountain through a tide of Nordic skate skiers on a training run from their school over the low hills through the woods behind the village and out onto the heavily traveled trail over the Golovin Bay ice to the neighboring village.

19

John Stewart

Miles before Scotsman John Stewart reached the Bering Sea coast, he knew his Iditarod was in trouble. At Old Woman cabin on the Kaltag Portage 35 miles short of Unalakleet, he could see his Iditarod dream dying, but he clung to the fragments of hope. He clearly wasn't going to show well in the race. There was already a growing chance the two women then at the tail end of the race – Celeste Davis from Montana and Jane Faulkner from Soldotna– might pass and relegate him to last. But Stewart planned to do his damnedest to reach Nome and collect that coveted belt buckle that goes to Iditarod finishers.

Warm inside the snug cabin of three-sided logs that the U.S. Bureau of Land Management built to replace the plywood Old Woman shack back down by the Unalakleet River, the 24-year-old laughed and joked with Montana musher Chris Adkins and Washington state's Scott White. Back in the corner, Idaho's Trent Herbst dozed quietly. A fourth-grade teacher with a bushy beard that hung to his chest and a ratty, rag wool stocking hat that never seemed to leave his head, Herbst was a veteran of three previous Iditarods. A native of the Midwest, his plan to run one Iditarod in 2006 had grown into many races after he hooked up with Nature's Kennel Sled Dog Adventures run by Ed and Tasha Stielstra in northern Michigan. The Steilstra's found in the 39-year-old man originally from next-door Wisconsin a first-class puppy trainer and marketing ally. Herbst took their dogs out on the Iditarod Trail to earn them an Iditarod cachet. Then he helped with some of the marketing for their sled dog business. A well-spoken musher who looked like a wild man form the north, Herbst keynoted the Midwest Iditarod Teacher's conference in 2010.

Herbst trail mate Chris Adkins was a 41-year-old Iditarod rookie whose association with the Iditarod went back in one way or another for most of his life. His father, Terry, was an Iditarod legend – the veterinarian for the very first Iditarod, the first Outside musher to crack the Iditarod top 10, a veteran of 20 races, a friend and once stand-in doctor for race founder Joe Redington Sr. Terry stitched up old Joe's knee in Skwentna one year because there were no doctors available. Both Chris and Terry now lived in Sand Coulee, Montana, and knew Stewart from there. The Scotsman had been living in the Big Sky state training with neighbor Doug Swingley.

White likewise knew the other men from races across the West. A designer for a construction company in Woodinville, he'd been running dogs for more than a decade and tried to spend as much time in Alaska as possible. He'd taken a shot at the Iditarod in 2007, but ran into that trouble in Rainy Pass. He got disoriented; his dogs got in a fight. White took his gloves off to try to straighten out his team in screaming winds and bitter cold, and he ended up seriously frostbiting his hands. He had to quit.

Still officially a rookie, he was back in 2010 older and wiser. Along with the others, he could laugh at the mistakes of the younger Stewart, who'd left the Iditarod restart in Willow hoping to run a top-20 race only to go too fast too far.

There is an old axiom in marathon running that says that for every mile run a minute too fast in the first half of a race there will be many minutes lost in the last half of the race. The same applies for the Iditarod. Dogs that go out too fast tend to gas out. Stewart left Skwentna behind a 12 mile-per-hour team. It was slowing down quickly by the time he reached the Interior. By the time he hit the coast, he'd be dropping tired dogs left and right while plodding behind a six mile-per-hour team. Fading and injured dogs, however, weren't his only problem. Stewart himself had been sick through much of the early part of the race.

"I was literally five minutes from scratching at Cripple because I felt so bad," he told Adkins and White. He was talked out of it by Cripple checkers – Drs. Bill and Jim Gallea, father and son. White spent 16 hours in Cripple resting as much as he could in a warm tent between forays out into the 30-to 50-degree-below-zero cold to feed dogs. The rest helped White and clearly did his dogs well. When they hit the trail to Ruby, the dogs made a 65-mile run at better than 11 miles per hour. Stewart might have let them go too fast again. At the riverside village, he had to drop three that had run too hard. The downward spiral that had started just before midway in the race was accelerating.

The young but experienced Scot had asked Swingley to pencil out a schedule for a 10-day Iditarod. The former champ obliged. It was more than Stewart and his team could handle, and by Old Woman he had begun to recognize that.

"I should have said 'puppy schedule,'" Stewart joked, "easy puppy schedule. I was 12 hours behind my schedule by Takotna."

It only got worse, and more painful, as the trail moved north. Fellow Scotsman Wattie MacDonald, 44, a large, happy-go-lucky man running a team on a more conservative schedule, was almost three hours behind Stewart when the race hit halfway at Cripple, but he'd been closing fast for two days. And when he left Cripple, he was five hours in front his younger countryman. Stewart would never come close to catching up.

"I envy Wattie with those 16 dogs cruising to Nome," Stewart said. "He's got those cyborg dogs. He doesn't have to do anything with them."

The dogs were out of the kennel of former Iditarod champ Dean Osmar from Clam Gulch. MacDonald, an oil field worker who keeps 11 Siberian huskies at home in Scotland, had raised and/or fished out of his pocket a reported $85,000 to lease the team. The Scotsman then invested the winter of 2009 qualifying to run Iditarod and the winter of 2010 training under the watchful eye of Osmar to make his Iditarod dream a reality. Once on the trail, the older Scotsman did a bang-up job of dog care. He was the only musher in the 2010 race to make Nome with 16 dogs still in harness.

MacDonald arrived there at the finish in 45th position, while Stewart was still on his way to White Mountain, 80 miles from the end. Though Stewart was able to joke about the drubbing he was getting at the paws of MacDonald's team, it was visibly not an easy thing for the young musher to endure. Despite his age, he's been at the sled dog game a lot longer than the older man.

MacDonald got his first husky in 1999. By that time, Stewart had been on the runners five years. He started when he was eight. His parents, Alan and Fiona, run the Cairngorm Dog Sled Centre on Rothiemurchus Estate in Scotland. John had been immersed in the mythology of Alaska sled dogs almost since birth. The family business included the only sled dog museum in Europe. There was a special section devoted to the legendary Alaska dog driver Allan Alexander "Scotty" Allan. Allan had been born and reared in Dundee, not far away from Stewart's home, before leaving for America at 19 to train horses and eventually chasing gold to the north in Alaska. It was there dog driver Scotty Allan and a scraggly mutt named "Baldy" bought in Nome became famous. Baldy three times led Allan teams to victories in the All Alaska Sweepstakes, then the biggest deal in North American sled dog racing. Results of the races made the New York Times in their day. Allan and Baldy were always in contention. Along with three victories, they claimed three seconds and two thirds. Allan became so well known and popular in Nome he was twice elected to the Alaska Territorial Legislature.

Like Allan, the Stewarts had a long association with dogs and were locally recognized. Among the small clique of dog mushers in the British Isles, the Stewarts were as well known as the likes of Jeff King and Martin Buser in Alaska. John himself was a Scottish and British sprint champion. A smallish man with an accent sometimes hard to understand

and the muscle tone of a professional athlete, John was a professional diver by trade. He worked beneath the oilrigs of the North Sea. It was a dangerous business, but it paid well. He used the money to help subsidize his sled dog addiction. When he wasn't underwater, he was running dogs.

Most of his races had been contested behind carts and not sleds, but he still had strong sled-driving credentials. He'd raced in South America. He'd worked for Anchorage Fur Rendezvous World Champion Egil Ellis in Alaska, for Yukon Quest International Sled Dog Race champion Hans Gatt in Canada, and Iditarod champ Swingley in Montana. And were this not enough, he and his father had helped pioneer sled dog cart rides for tourists in Jamaica. That eventually led to the birth of the Jamaica Dogsled Team, sponsored by singer Jimmy Buffett, and the rise of Jamaican musher Newton Marshall, 27. Marshall was a big story in Iditarod 2010. He grabbed international headlines as a black man from the tropics competing in an event dominated by white men from the frozen north.

There were no headlines for John. And, unlike Marshall, who pretty much laughed his way north from Willow to finish the race in 47th place, there wasn't much joy for John, either, except when he could laugh at the absurdity of it all.

"I'm scared of everyone frowning on me," he joked as he gobbled a big meal in the Yupik Eskimo village of Koyuk. "If (Doug Swingley) is there in Nome, I might turn the team right around on Front Street."

By Koyuk, John was the last Swingley musher standing. Two others running Swingley dogs – Warren Palfrey from Quesnel, B.C., Canada, and Tom Thurston from Oak Creek, Colo. – had already scratched. Stewart worried about what Swingley might be thinking. The Scotsman was of the opinion he'd taken a great looking dog team and made a mess of it.

"It's hard on a human that you've got to look at those dogs when they're going through those uncomfortable spells," he said. "I'm used to happy dogs."

In front of him as the race moved up the coast were some unhappy trudgers. He was playing babysitter and cheerleader as he tried to left their spirits, hoping they could get to Nome. It wasn't an easy task. Coming across Norton Bay to Koyuk, he confessed, there were a couple times his once lively, happy dog team looked to be struggling so that "I nearly cried. I'm sorry for my dog team. They were underprepared. I'm down to eight dogs. That's not good."

None of the eight were yapping and lunging at their harnesses when he stopped on the trail anymore, either. They sort of just stood around until he told them to go and then they slogged forward. Swingley warned that there would be times when the dogs wouldn't seem particularly happy. As with human marathoners and ultra marathoners, dogs in the Iditarod go through all sorts of mood swings from beginning to end. John was told not to judge things by their attitudes over a few hours but by their behavior over a day or more.

All the musher was seeing by the coast, though, were the low points. That only added to his problem. Dog mushers and their teams develop strong emotional connections. It is easy for the depression of the musher to spread to the dogs.

In this case, the defeat showing in Stewart's team seemed to be infecting the man, and that in term was affecting the dogs. It was a bad feedback loop.

It would, finally and absolutely, come to an end in White Mountain. Down to six dogs by then, the freckle-faced Stewart was told by veterinarians that Eltoro, a lead dog and team mainstay, would have to be dropped. It was the last straw.

Stewart couldn't go on. Until he got that news, he'd hung in. Fit and small, willing to run up every hill behind the sled, a sort of Scottish version of champ Jeff King, he'd started the Iditarod with the hope that he'd win the "entry fee back and, hopefully, pick something else up," as he told his local newspaper, the Strathspey & Badenoch Herald. When that dream faded away, he refocused on trying to beat MacDonald. When that benchmark fell, he committed himself to simply getting the belt buckle awarded those who finish. He'd invested $40,000 and a big chunk of his heart in the Iditarod dream.

"It's an expensive belt buckle," he admitted, but better than nothing. He had all of his belt-buckle hopes invested in Eltoro as the race neared the end. And Eltoro was game until he dragged the rest of the team up and over the 1,000-foot mountain mushers call "Little McKinley" to White Mountain on soft trail in the heat of the day. Eltoro got the team into the next checkpoint, but he was spent.

The realization that Eltoro couldn't go on was a psychological blow too big for Stewart to endure. As the last teams of Iditarod 2010 left for the Nome finish line, the young musher threw in the towel and went to console his ailing lead dog.

"It's for the best," he said, "but it will be debatable if I come back."

Stung by an Alaska Range ground blizzard, brutalized by 50-degree-below-zero Innoko River cold, slapped around by Yukon River winds, a young and intelligent Stewart had realized the madness of the Iditarod just might not be his thing. There were other races. The shorter ones, he thought, might be better suited to his style.

"This was only my fourth long distance race," he said. "You gotta try it once."

He might have taken heart that Scotty Allan's big event, The All Alaska Sweepstakes, the biggest sled dog race in the north in the early 1900s, was a 400 miler. Four hundred miles is less than half an Iditarod. And upon arrival at halfway in Iditarod 2010, Stewart was still in front of old Wattie MacDonald.

20

Safety to Nome

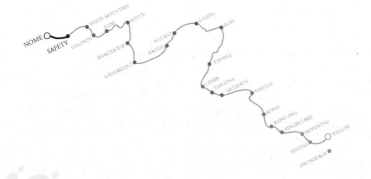

Once the cold of winter freezes Safety Lagoon and the snow begins to pile high on the barrier beaches along Norton Sound, the landscape east of Nome turns almost lunar. Safety Roadhouse, 20 miles from the Iditarod finish, looms like a moon station. Rising on pilings above a sea of white, it is an outpost in a lifeless land. Miles ahead along the Iditarod Trail, the immensity of 300-foot-high, mile-long Cape Nome appears a beached whale. To the south, snow-covered ice hides the bay and the landscape stretches toward the even greater nothingness of the frozen Bering Sea. Back down the trail to the east toward the ghost town of Solomon, there is a frozen emptiness that the eye follows into the rolling hills that lead to the equally great emptiness of the Seward Peninsula.

Some years there is visible a hint of the bridge that

carries the Nome-Council Road across the entrance to the Sound about a quarter mile east of the roadhouse, but in 2010 there was so much snow the road itself was invisible and the bridge nearly so. The 25-by-50-foot roadhouse stood as lonely as a desert garrison with only the occasional movement outside of a passing dog team, the checkpoint veterinarian, the Iditarod checker or the rare checkpoint visitors.

Once, back in the golden days of Alaska's mining boom, there had been a community here. Mamie Maloney, whose father owned the roadhouse from 1910 to 1951, told a historian for the Iditarod National Historic Trail that once the roadhouse was surrounded by a lot of "little cabins." The cabins, she added, floated away in flood. The first roadhouse burned down, too, she said. But it was rebuilt prior to 1913, and that old structures still stands. It has seen a lot of Alaska history.

The Safety Roadhouse is the last stop for Iditarod mushers as they march toward Nome. It's the place where mushing history has been made, where dramatic strategies between competitors have unfolded, and where the race can still be lost. Long before daughter-of-Alaska and former governor Sarah Palin became a national celebrity, the roadhouse played a role in the creation of two national celebrities – dog musher Gunnar Kaasen and his lead dog, Balto. They starred in the diphtheria serum run of 1925.

The diphtheria outbreak in Nome threatened every resident, but bad weather grounded airplanes and extreme cold kept the horses that normally carried mail north to the city in their barns. Health officials called on dog mushers and their teams to ferry life-saving diphtheria serum for more than 600 miles from the train station at Nenana down the Tanana River to the Yukon, and down the Yukon to connect with the Iditarod Trail and on to Nome. Most of the dog drivers in the serum run hurried their life-saving, 20-pound load only 25 to 45 miles along the trail before handing it off, but two mushers went significantly farther: Kassen and Leonard Seppala. And what happened at Safety became pivotal in the telling and retelling of the story of the great diphtheria serum run to Nome.

Seppala and lead dog Togo already were Alaska mushing legends when the serum run began. If anyone could help save Nome, it was that duo. So with death stalking the streets, Seppala left the city on Jan. 27, 1925 and headed out to meet dog drivers already hurrying vital serum north.

The weather was brutal – 30 degrees below zero with gale force winds that pushed wind chill temperatures to 85 degrees below. Seppala, Togo and the team pushed on anyway. On Jan. 31, about 200 miles from Nome near Shaktoolik, they met Henry Ivanoff fighting his way north through the same weather. Seppala took the serum from Ivanoff and told him to go back to the safety of the village. Then Seppala, risking his life and that of his team, turned back the way he had come and fought across the exposed ice of Norton Sound toward Nome.

On Feb. 1, with 40-degree-below-zero temperatures and 65-mile-per-hour winds engulfing the region, a bone weary Seppala handed the serum to Charlie Olson at 3 p.m. in Golovin even as the storm worsened.

Olsen headed out into the blizzard unaware that authorities had ordered the relay stopped. They feared the loss of musher and serum in the blow. But phone lines were down and their command to halt never arrived. Olsen charged ahead on a nightmare run. When he stopped to try to put protective blankets on his dogs, he severely frostbit his hands. He did not turn back, however, but kept going and reached the mining camp at Bluff. There he gave the serum to Kaasen who waited a while for the storm to ease, but when it showed no sign of doing so set out for Solomon.

Lead dog Balto – a second-string dog in Seppala's kennel – led Kaasen's team through the treacherous Topkok Hills, but with the winds so severe Kaasen sometimes couldn't see his team, he missed Solomon and drove on toward Safety.

At Safety, Ed Rohn was the dog driver waiting to ferry the serum on the last leg of the relay to Nome. He later claimed he was ready there and the signal light had been lit to indicate a relay driver was in place. But Kassen bypassed the last stop at Safety. He said his team was moving strong when he got there; everyone at Safety seemed to be sleeping; and, it seemed faster to keep going than to try and get another driver up and ready his team.

Whether Kaasen made the move to grab glory has never been determined with certainty. What is known is that Kassen was the musher who brought the serum into Nome and got the credit for saving the city. He ended up collecting a $1,000 award from the Territory of Alaska while the other 19 mushers in the "Great Race of Mercy" received $25 each. Both Kaasen and Balto became national celebrities for their life-saving efforts. New York City put up a statue in Central Park to honor Balto the "wonder dog." Kaasen starred in the movie "Balto's Race to Nome" and toured the West with his dog team, while some in Nome steamed over the thought the wrong dog and the wrong musher got credit for saving their community from an epidemic. The locals thought more credit should have gone to two icons of the north – dog musher Seppala and his race-winning lead dog Togo.

Togo, however, wasn't totally overlooked. Seppala took the dog on a cross-country tour in 1926, during which Togo spent 10 days as the featured attraction at Madison Square Garden. Arctic explorer Roald Amundsen gave the dog a gold medal. And after Togo's death three years later, Seppala had him made into a full-size, lifelike mount, which now resides in a glass display case at the Iditarod museum in Wasilla.

The Safety Roadhouse, meanwhile, continued to play a key role in Alaska history. Maloney was there with an Eskimo babysitter in 1931 when an airplane on pontoons circled overhead and then landed on the nearby lagoon. The babysitter, terrified by the noise of the new-fangled contraption in the air, hid under a bed, Maloney said in her 1980 interview with federal historians. At that very moment, the roadhouse phone started ringing. Maloney answered to find someone wanting to know if Charles Lindbergh, the famous aviator, was in Safety. Then came a knock at the door. Maloney answered, and there was Lindbergh. She took him the phone, she recalled, and said, "It's for you." And he looked at me like 'How do you know who I am?'" She knew who he was because everyone in Nome knew who he was. The Lindberghs, Charles and wife, Ann, were due there on a pioneering flight to the Orient. Anne Morrow Lindbergh later wrote a book about the adventure, "North to the Orient" while Safety quieted down for a few years. That changed with the birth of the

Iditarod Trail Sled Dog Race in 1973.

In Iditarod lore, Safety is the place where mushers Dick Mackey from Wasilla and Rick Swenson, then from Eureka, came through neck-and-neck in 1978 dueling their way to Nome. Mackey eventually won in the Iditarod's only photo finish. Swenson's dog sled crossed the line first, but victory went to Mackey – the father of future champs Lance and Rick – because he was the musher behind the first dog to cross the line.

Nine years later, Swenson played a part in another drama that unfolded at Safety, but capitulated to archrival Susan Butcher after his dogs lay down and refused to leave the checkpoint. What had been a cat-and-mouse duel between the one-time neighbors all the way up the coast ended with Swenson walking into the roadhouse, slapping a bill on the counter, and ordering a Coke with a shot of whiskey.

It was the worst of times for the old dog lover from Two Rivers, but the best of times would come for Swenson at Safety in 1991. He was that year the fourth musher out of White Mountain behind Butcher, Runyan and Tim Osmar, a former Junior Iditarod champ from Clam Gulch. The weather was horrible. Not quite serum run bad, but bad. Butcher, Runyan and Osmar eventually turned their teams back for the safety of the White Mountain checkpoint. Swenson kept going. He walked much of the way through the Topkok Hills at the front of the team to find the trail. He put his thickest-skinned dogs in coats on the windward side of his team to shelter their teammates in the lee. He was, he said, later worried about his own survival a few times, but figured that just as long as the team didn't lose the trail, they'd survive.

Swenson emerged from the storm at Safety. He blew on through the checkpoint to grab his fifth Iditarod victory. That is how mushers want to pass through Safety – in and out quickly – on the way to the finish, but it doesn't always happen that way. Fairbank's Judy Currier, a University of New Hampshire-educated veteran of two Iditarods by 2006, had her dogs quit four miles out of the Safety checkpoint that year, and watched her early-race hopes of becoming another Lance Mackey go poof. Her race had looked so good early on, too. Ninth behind four-time Iditarod champ Swingley at the Cripple halfway point, she started falling off the pace thereafter and kept falling and falling and falling. She was all the way back in 41st position by the time her dogs laid down short of Safety.

She managed to get them up, get in front and walk them into the checkpoint, and there they sat for almost 24 hours. Currier watched 11 teams go past. Physically, the veterinarian at the checkpoint said, her dogs were fine. Mentally, they'd had enough. They eventually recovered and went on to Nome, but Currier's hoped for top 10 finish turned into 53rd. It was almost worse for Scott White.

The musher, whose first try at the Iditarod in 2007 ended with frostbitten fingers at Rainy Pass, thought he had it made at White Mountain on his second attempt. His dogs looked solid, and after the mandatory eight-hour rest at the penultimate checkpoint they trotted over the Topkok Hills at a steady seven miles per hour. They should have blown right through Safety, as most teams do, and gone on to Nome. Nobody pauses at Safety except to drop a tired dog slowing the team. White, however, dawdled just a little too long signing the check-in sheet and looking around the roadhouse. His dogs lay down and waited. They had grown accustomed to stopping at checkpoints. They were used to eating and napping in such places, and so they decided to do just that in Safety. White got them up, but they didn't want to go. He walked them out on the trail to Nome. They followed along quite contentedly behind, but they were unwilling to let him ride. White no longer had a functioning dog team. So he turned around and walked the dogs back to Safety. There he went through the checkpoint ritual. He cooked dog food. He fed the team. He let them rest. Four hours later, they all headed off toward Nome. Everything looked to be fine, but it wasn't.

"They stopped in the exact same spot we'd turned around before," White said. So, once more, he walked the team back to Safety. He snacked them. He bedded them down again. He went into the roadhouse, admired all the signed dollar bills tacked to the walls and looked over the bar, which was closed. The Iditarod in 2010 was cracking down on drinking along the trail, along with drug testing mushers for the first time ever. Unable even to get a drink, White sat dejectedly on the sofa next to the pool table in the bar's little lounge.

Friend Chris Atkins from Sand Coulee, Montana, went past outside riding behind his dog team bound for Nome. So did Dave DeCaro from Denali Park and Ross Adam. White was lower than his dogs when Adam, an Alberta buffalo rancher enjoying a camping trip to Nome behind a fast bunch of young dogs, blew through the checkpoint. It only got worse when Soldotna's Jane Faulkner, who'd once been a day behind White, and was at that point the second-to-last musher in Iditarod, showed up. White got up from the sofa to see her in and out and then he went back and plopped down dejected.

"This isn't the way it was supposed to turn out," he said.

And, in the end, it wasn't the way it turned out. A snow-machiner arriving at Safety pointed out to White that it was only 20 miles to Nome. A man can walk that far in good weather easy enough if he really wants to finish the Iditarod. If the dogs were willing to follow, the snowmachiner suggested, White should get out in front of them and start hiking to the finish. With just a little luck, the musher was reminded, the dogs would probably get tired of poking along at man pace and go on by, offering the driver a chance to jump the sled. White thought about the suggestions for a while. Then he put a leash on one of his leaders and started off on a long walk. The dogs followed.

The whole bunch was plodding toward the base of Cape Nome when Montanan Celeste Davis – the last musher still in the race – reached the roadhouse and signed through. For a time, it looked like she might catch White and pass the red lantern to him. White, meanwhile, was wondering if he would, indeed, walk all the way to Nome. He'd hoped the dogs would pick up steam at the top of the cape, but they didn't. Only the sled did. Coming downhill, it wanted to overrun the dogs. White had to stop and throw out his snowhooks to drag behind to hold the sled back.

Another snowmachiner, seeing this, stopped to tell White how lucky he was to have the snowhooks designed by a friend. Those particular snowhooks, the snowmachiner noted, were designed so that if a sled got loose they would automatically flip over to imbed their points in the ground and stop the team. White was testimony to the idea the design was better in theory than in practice, but that was fine with him. In practice, at least at walking speed, the hooks dragged along with the points aimed at the sky, which was just enough to slow the sled but not enough to stop it. White didn't want it stopped. He wanted it slowed down enough to stay behind the dogs until they decided to go faster than man-walking speed.

Eventually, they did. Part way down Cape Nome, White's dogs passed him and he jumped the sled. By the time the team hit the bottom of the hill and started along the last stretch of beach to the City of the Golden Sands, White, miraculously, had a dog team back. His dogs were out of their funk and suddenly racing for the finish line. They beat Davis there by 45 minutes.

White was mighty happy and more than a little relieved. After two tries, a huge effort, and a pile of money, he'd finally earned himself a belt buckle.

21

The End of the Trail

Broken-nosed Celeste Davis should never have made the finish line of the 2010 Iditarod Trail Sled Dog Race. Nurse Jane Faulkner and her sometimes leaderless team probably shouldn't have made it, either. Scott White almost didn't make it after his team decided that 980 miles was quite enough.

All three were Iditarod rookies. All three made rookie mistakes and suffered rookie errors. Of the bunch, Faulkner should have known better. Three times she went to Nome as part of the Norman Vaughan Serum Run. It doesn't exactly follow the entire route of the Iditarod, but it follows much of it and covers almost 700 miles from Nenana in the Interior to the Bering Sea coast.

This was the route used to rush the life-saving diphtheria serum from Anchorage to Nome in 1925. The Alaska Railroad hauled the serum from tidewater to the river port south of Fairbanks and the teams of mushers shuttled it north. The Serum Run event first organized by the late Norman Vaughan reenacts this noble mission of life and death, but it is not a race.

As Faulkner was to learn, as many before her have

learned, there is a difference between traveling cross-country – no matter how you travel – and racing cross-country. An experienced bicycle racer, Faulkner probably should have known this, but somehow she forgot.

"I didn't know Iditarod was going to be as hard as it is," she said, sitting in the warm, quiet Old Woman cabin on the Kaltag Portage more than three-quarters of the way through the race. "We cruised through this on the Serum Run."

Faulkner was at Old Woman with Davis this time. They were dirty and tired and joking and laughing. They'd become jovial trail mates, and at that point deep into the 1,000-mile race to Nome, they could sense the culmination of a dream in their grasp.

How or why is hard to explain. There was no logical reason for the newfound confidence. Only 60 or 70 miles or so back down the trail on the Yukon River, Faulkner had been dejected and demoralized. The on-again, off-again collection of pets in front of her sled was off again.

That they would make Nome was at best a "maybe," but the Iditarod is a world of maybes. Maybe the dogs will get stronger; maybe they won't. Maybe the wind clogging the eyes of team and the driver with blowing snow will stop; maybe it won't. Maybe the brutal cold will break; maybe it won't. Maybe tomorrow a musher will feel better about the journey; maybe she won't.

There is a lot of raw emotion out on the trail. For some Iditarod mushers, that turns into a good reason never to come back. For others, it is the reason they can't stay away. For some, it is both.

"It's too expensive," Faulkner said. "I told Randy (her

boyfriend), 'Don't ever let me do this again.'"

Unspoken was the knowledge that she wouldn't need to tell him to stop her from doing Iditarod again unless there was a danger she might do it again. Never mind that she'd put herself in debt to do Iditarod 2010. Never mind that she, like so many others, had suffered an Iditarod ordeal. Never mind the frostbite on the ends of her fingers. Never mind the exhausting double life of emergency room nurse at Central Peninsula Hospital in Soldotna and sled dog trainer on the trails of the Kenai. It is hard to explain to the uninitiated the focus required to maintain this double life.

Burt Bomhoff, a former president of the Iditarod Trail Committee, did the same thing in Southcentral Alaska for more than 20 years. Then one day he came home from work tired and wanting to enjoy a glass of wine after dinner only to realize he couldn't let himself have a drink. He might relax and neglect to get on the runners of the dog sled to take those dogs out on their nightly training run. That was the beginning of the end of his mushing career.

Mushers don't really own sled dogs as much as they are owned by them and their Iditarod dreams. Davis couldn't let go of the dream even after it knocked her cuckoo. Only two days into the 2010 Iditarod, she broke her nose, smashed her face, gushed blood all over the trail, and yet never thought about quitting. After the accident, her first thought was not about herself but about the safety of her team. She only thought about herself in the context of the dogs. If she bled to death, none of them would make Nome. It was in this moment, too, that she met the woman who would help her reach the finish – Faulkner – and the woman she would help reach the finish – the same Faulkner.

"She was behind me," Davis said, "and she helped me get my sled unhooked from the tree." A friendship soon formed. Faulkner for days offered moral support and sometimes a little more to the woman with the badly swollen face and what were to become two black eyes. Later, on the Yukon when Faulkner's dogs started to waver, Davis would return the favor. She would put her team in front of Faulkner's to give the lagging dogs something to chase.

It was more than a little amazing she was there to do that. The shift in her personality after the Dalzell crash was symptomatic of a significant concussion. It might have gone unnoticed because Davis's face was so badly smashed no one really wanted to look at her. People avoided eye contact for fear they might be caught staring at the woman with the blue, swollen face and the brown, blondish hair tied up in corn rows. Her injury was visibly worse than that which had caused the emergency evacuation of musher Pat Moon by airplane. He had a gash on his face after hitting a tree. Davis had a face that had been rearranged.

"It rocked my world," she admitted later. "I'd never feared anything before."

After the accident, she feared something. She feared she might be forced to drop out of the Iditarod. The fact her nose was smashed? Well, she didn't seem to fear that at all. She merely felt sorry for her 11-year-old son, Beau, who would welcome home a mommy who looked even worse than when she left.

Davis was able to joke about the injury because she is an attractive woman reared in one of those Western environs where appearance doesn't matter all that much. It wasn't like she'd spent her youth getting prettied up to go to debutante balls. Instead, her childhood had gone to the dogs.

Her first trip along Alaska's fabled Iditarod Trail was the culmination of that life. If the dogs were good to go, she was good to go; and it really didn't matter how bad she looked or felt.

The journey did get better, too. The swelling in her face went down to the point her nose was swollen, not grotesque, although her black eyes did give her a raccoon-like mask that helped to make Davis's face one of the most photographed of Iditarod 2010. "I felt like a celebrity there for a while," she said. A checker at White Mountain late in the race greeted her with the pronouncement that "your reputation precedes you."

By then, both she and Faulkner were thrilled to have the end of the race in sight. They had caught Scotsman John Stewart, who Davis knew from the Montana racing scene, and they chatted him up in the penultimate checkpoint only 80 miles from Nome. They did not know at that point, as they all waited out a mandatory eight-hour rest for their teams, that Stewart would eventually scratch. He was then still hopeful of going on.

Davis and Faulkner knew, though, they had it made. The weather was cooperative. The dogs were willing. It was just a matter of the hiking over the Topkok Hills, and on to Nome to bring the Iditarod to an end.

"I've been working my ass off to get that red lantern," Davis joked over breakfast in White Mountain. "I'm ready to get the hell out of here."

"I brought a Scottish flag to wave (at the finish)," Stewart said. "Maybe I should have brought a white flag."

"You know, I'm so glad I've done this," Faulkner said.

Then both of the women started giggling. It was 6 a.m. in the morning. They were eating pizza for breakfast. They were dirty. They were tired. And they were patting themselves on the back for having accomplished something they hadn't yet accomplished.

"I don't even want to eat," Faulkner said, looking at the pizza. "I'm forcing myself to eat."

"My noses whistles when I breathe," Davis said.

They giggled some more, a couple of nurses – Davis, 37, Faulkner, 49 – behaving like schoolgirls in their sleep-deprived goofiness. Someone asked Faulkner if she wanted to take a shower before she left. She looked at her dirty hands, cracked and swollen after almost two weeks on the trail with frostbite blisters on the tips that she'd been debating for days whether to drain.

"I don't want to shower here," she said. "I'll do it in Nome."

Then she and Davis wandered down to the Fish River to ready their teams. Nine-year-old Ash, a dog that had tried twice before to make it to Nome without success, was stiff after the long rest. Faulkner took her for a walk on a leash to loosen up and petted her. She wanted the dog to finally see the Iditarod finish line. Davis got her dogs and lined them out in front of her sled.

"We're not going to win any money," Faulkner said. "We might as well have a good time."

Then the two women headed up the river. Three miles later, where the trail turned off toward the Topkoks, Faulkner's dogs broke into a lope, Ash along with the rest. The team that had seemed reluctant to go at times now seemed hell-bent on making Nome. They quickly left Davis behind. She was content to chug on alone, admiring the scenery on a day when the Alaska coast was unbelievably friendly.

The trail dipped and climbed through the history-rich Seward Peninsula. The last trees fell behind at a place called Timber on the way to the top of Topkok Head. There began a winding 500-foot descent to the beaches along the coast. Behind was the notorious "Blowhole" that has rocked many a sled and nearly killed a musher; it had been quiet and friendly for almost the entire race.

At the bottom of the hill, the trail rounded the Nome Kennel Club cabin that has saved countless mushers and snowmachiners from the storms of years past and headed straight toward the old Safety Roadhouse only 25 miles ahead. That's where White sat dejected, 20 miles from the finish line, wondering if he'd come this far only to see his Iditarod end in infamy. When Faulkner saw his team parked there, she knew instantly what had happened. She did not linger to make small talk. She did not want her dogs getting the idea that Safety was a real checkpoint. She signed the check-in sheet as quick as she could and was gone.

Faulkner was out of sight by the time Davis arrived. White and his team had started their walk and were visible miles to the west. Davis, like Faulkner, went through Safety in pursuit of the musher ahead though she really didn't want to catch him. She had her eyes on that red lantern as its own trophy of sorts.

And she collected it. Forty-five minutes after White arrived in Nome, Davis followed her dogs under the burled arch on Front Street. She'd been 13 days, 5 hours and 6 minutes on the trail from Willow. Her finishing time shattered the previous best for a red lantern winner. She took a full day off the standard set by Alaskan David Straub in 2002 on a trail so good race winner Martin Buser set an Iditarod record for a finishing time, which still stands. Davis could note her finish, though last, was fast enough to have won all of the Iditarods prior to 1981 and 11 of the 13 staged between 1973 and 1985 when Libby Riddles rocked the world by becoming the first woman ever to claim victory. Davis was happy and satisfied.

A week later, she was feted in her hometown of Deer Lodge, Montana. There was a parade down Main Street for her and lead dog, Teddy. A fire truck led the way. School children cheered from the corners, according to her hometown newspaper, the Silver State Post, which made front-page news of the celebration.

"The flashing sign on Peoples Bank cheered, 'Teddy and Celeste, Two Great Girls,'" the newspaper reported. "Mayor Mary Ann Fraley declared March 29, 2010 Celeste Davis Day for her courage and determination in finishing the 1,000-mile race."

The story, which was accompanied by a photo of Davis getting a smooch from musher father Bill Smith, took up a third of the front page. Davis had a red lantern beside her in the photo. She signed red lanterns later in the parking lot at Valley Foods. Her mother shed tears of pride. The broken nose was all but forgotten, and the black eyes had almost gone away. This was the happiest of happy endings.

Behind her though, was a trail of broken dreams. What separated the failures of the broken-hearted from the success of the broken-nosed musher who gave son Beau a ride on her sled down Nome's Front Street is hard to say. Of the 16 who didn't make it to the end, it could be said Davis was luckier than some and more committed than others. Half a dozen veterans dropped out after deciding that just finishing wasn't enough. They'd set goals they clearly weren't going to reach and rather than come up short they abandoned the race all together.

Several other mushers were punched out by the trail. Pat Moon hit that tree head high with his face and had to be evacuated. Michael Suprenant did the same only at trail level as he was being dragged behind a tipped-over sled; he was told to go home and heal his concussion. Judy Currier's bad back just couldn't take the pounding from endless miles of bad trail, and she gave it up.

Davis might have given it up, too, if not for the encouragement at some point of Faulkner. The same could be said in reverse. They were two women on a mission, sisters in adventure, the Thelma and Louise of the Iditarod Trail. They had a lot in common. Both were nurses. Both were mothers of only children. Both had a fondness for animals that had kept them in the sled dog game for a long time. Both loved to laugh. And both believed that, by God, come hell or high water, they were going to get to Nome.

And they did. They danced through the Graveyard of Dreams. They earned their belt buckles. They joined a very select club. They became veterans of the Iditarod Trail. They earned a distinction no one can ever take away.

About the Author

Craig Medred is an award-winning journalist and a contributor to the Alaska Dispatch. He has spent 30 years writing about the majesty and the extremes of Alaska. As the former Outdoor Editor for the Anchorage Daily News, he covered 25 consecutive Iditarods from Anchorage to Nome and has won numerous awards for his reporting. In 1987, he won the Best Newspaper Writing award for deadline writing from the American Society of Newspaper Editors [ASNE] for his Iditarod coverage. In detailing Medred's style, ASNE editors said: "Craig writes in a transparent voice that never calls attention to itself, letting the colorful characters of the mushers shine through unimpeded by his style." In 1992, he was named one of the best sports writers in America for his coverage of Iditarod mushers and the drama of the race across the Alaska tundra.

Originally from Staples, Minnesota, Medred moved to Alaska in 1973 where he earned a degree in journalism from the University of Alaska Fairbanks. He worked briefly in Washington, DC as the press secretary to then-Senator Mike Gravel, but has spent most of his career in broadcast and newspaper journalism.

Medred is an outdoor enthusiast who loves to fish, hunt, ski, mountain bike and chase Alaska adventures in a half dozen other ways. He and his family, including two labrador retrievers and a West Highland Terrier, live in Anchorage, Alaska.